Straight Talk About Post-Traumatic Stress Disorder

Coping with the Aftermath of Trauma

Kay Marie Porterfield

☑ Facts On File®

AN INFOBASE HOLDINGS COMPANY

Straight Talk About Post-Traumatic Stress Disorder: Coping with the Aftermath of Trauma

Facts On File, Inc.
11 Penn Plaza
New York, NY 10001

Library of Congress Cataloging-in-Publication Data

Porterfield, Kay Marie.
   Straight talk about post-traumatic stress disorder : coping with the aftermath of trauma / Kay Marie Porterfield.
      p. cm.
   Includes bibliographical references and index.
   Summary: An in-depth discussion of the condition known to psychologists as post-traumatic stress disorder or PTSD, including possible causes, symptoms, treatment, the process of recovery, and sources of help.
   ISBN 0-8160-3258-0 (hb : alk. paper)
   ISBN 0-8160-3552-0 (pb : alk. paper)
   1. Post-traumatic stress disorder. [1. Post-traumatic stress disorder.]   I. Title.
RC552.P67P65 1996
616.85'21—dc20 95-21006

Facts On File books are available at special discounts when purchased in bulk quantities for businesses, associations, institutions or sales promotions. Please call our Special Sales Department in New York at 212/967-8800 or 800/322-8755.

Jacket design by Dorothy Wachtenheim

Printed in the United States of America

MP FOF 10 9 8 7 6 5 4 3 2 1

This book is printed on acid-free paper.

Straight Talk About Post-Traumatic Stress Disorder

Other Titles for Teenagers by the Author

Contents

About the Straight Talk About . . . series:
The Straight Talk About . . . books provide young adult readers with the most factual, up-to-date information available. Recognizing that the teen years are a time of growth and transition, the authors aim not to dispense any easy answers or moral judgments but to help young people clarify a number of issues and difficult choices and to consider the consequences of their decisions. Each book is thorougly indexed and contains a directory of resources.

Straight Talk About Post-Traumatic Stress Disorder

1

Scarred Minds, Shattered Lives: Living with the Aftermath of Trauma

As you read the following stories about events in the lives of other teenagers, think about whether something like what happened to them has ever happened to you or to someone you know. How are your experiences or those of your friends similar to the ones described below? How do they differ?

When Bill* was walking the four blocks home from studying at a friend's house one evening, he heard footsteps behind him. He picked up his pace, but the teenagers that had been

---

*Everyone identified by first name only in this book is a composite—a portrait drawn from details that come from many different people.

following him charged forward, surrounding him.   The minute he saw their gang colors, he was more frightened than ever before in his life. They took his watch and his money—less than five dollars—but still they weren't satisfied. Before he knew what was happening, he was on the ground desperately fighting off punches and kicks. Fortunately, Bill's tormentors soon tired of their game.

During the several days it took for his cuts and bruises to heal, Bill vowed not to let the gang members intimidate him.   Instead, he seemed to successfully put the ugly incident behind him and even continued walking home from his friend's alone at night. His life seemed so normal that he was surprised when four months later, he found he couldn't sleep without a light on. Soon even that didn't work. At school he began sitting in the corner, his back against the wall, where he could keep an eye on everyone, just in case someone tried something funny. By the end of the semester, he had failed two classes. He'd lost friends, too. Instead of being his usual outgoing self, now he was suddenly moody and irritable. If a classmate walked up behind him in the hallway, he jumped, immediately ready to fight or run. He told himself that, since he trusted no one, he didn't really care that his old friends stopped spending time with him. Deep down, though, his loneliness really hurt.

When Paul, who sat across from Rayetta in math class, started flirting with her, she wanted to be able to talk to him like her friends did to the boys who liked them. Yet something seemed to stop her from even being able to look at him when he dropped hints about wanting to take her to a movie. Her reluctance was more than shyness. All Paul had to do was smile in a certain way, and her muscles tensed so much that she sat frozen while fear and rage battled inside of her. As the teacher droned on about percentages and multiplying fractions, Rayetta alternated between wanting to throw up, bolt from the room, or start pounding on poor Paul, whom she'd enjoyed joking around with when he had just wanted to be a friend.

Soon afterward the dreams started—nightmares about a dark, shadowy man who crept into her bedroom, ripped off her nightgown, fought with her, and tried to choke her. Always it was the same nightmare over and over, so vivid she woke up shaking and sick to her stomach. In the dream she was a little girl and could *almost* make out the identity of the attacker. He was someone she'd known; she was sure of that much. But who?

Even worse were the occasions in her daily life when she thought she recognized the man from her dream. Most of the time, she managed to hide the fear that shot through her when she caught a glimpse of someone who reminded her of him. Once, though, when she'd gone with her friends to a video arcade at the neighborhood mall, the dream images had begun to flash through her mind like a horror movie she was condemned to watch. As she smelled the nightmare man's sour odor and felt his sweaty body pushing against hers in this flashback, she started to hyperventilate. When her friends asked her what was wrong, she couldn't answer. Instead she had run all the way home, her lungs nearly bursting, and locked herself in her room. Was she going crazy? Sometimes she thought so. What was happening made no sense to her at all.

When the apartment in which Karen and her family had lived burned down, nobody had been hurt except for her kitten, who had died. Even so, Karen had been scared to death, standing barefoot in the snow, wearing nothing but an extra-large T-shirt, and watching firemen battle the hot, orange flames. The scene had reminded her of the pictures of hell that her grandpa had liked to paint to frighten her into behaving as a child.

Someone brought her a wooly blanket to wrap herself in and a pair of men's running shoes. The Red Cross got a motel room for her mother, her sisters, and herself that night. There was no luggage to carry when they checked in because they'd lost everything—family pictures, their important papers, clothes, furniture, all of Karen's stuffed animals, and her artwork. Not even a scrap of paper remained to remind her of the past 13 years that she'd been alive. It was as if God had taken a big ax and chopped the past away completely.

Within a matter of weeks the family was settled in a new apartment, a much nicer place to live than the old one. Friends and neighbors were great about donating clothing and money to the family, and Karen's mother had a good job, so she was able to come up with a down payment for brand-new furniture. In many ways their lives were better than before the fire.

"We need to be thankful we're all safe and get on with the business of living," her mom kept saying, but Karen didn't feel much gratitude. She missed her old life, and she missed her cat. At the same time she didn't feel really sad. In fact, she never cried about what had happened. Numb was more like what she felt—cold and dead inside, as if the fire had burned up something inside of her and all that remained were the cold, gray ashes. She started keeping to herself, sitting in her darkened room and trying to think of as many ways as she could to get out alive if this new apartment caught fire.

Bill, Rayetta, and Karen were relatively happy and well-adjusted until one day, in the blink of an eye, their lives were turned upside down when an unexpected event that was completely beyond their control happened to them. As a result, their lives are now deeply affected by a collection of disturbing symptoms that psychologists have come to call *post-traumatic stress disorder,* or *PTSD* for short.

According to the American Psychiatric Association's definition, PTSD is a feeling of marked terror or helplessness and is accompanied by a set of characteristic symptoms that follow a distressing event, called a *trauma,* that is outside the range of usual human experience.

A recent example of such an event with far-reaching impact is the bombing of the Federal Center in Oklahoma City in April of 1995. One had only to view the shaken faces of survivors, victims' family members, and rescue workers shown on television to begin to understand how strongly something so upsetting affects those it touches. Even people who weren't in or near the building, but who watched news reports, found themselves afraid that something just as terrible might unexpectedly happen to them or someone they knew. They were outraged, as well, at the people who had blown up the building and killed so many people. Suddenly the world no longer seemed a safe place.

The symptoms of PTSD disappear in time without any treatment for some people. For others, life improves with therapy, but the symptoms continue to linger to some extent for a lifetime. Some people, like Bill and Rayetta, have delayed signs of PTSD, which do not surface until months or years after the traumatic event.

PTSD can occur at any age, even during childhood, and it can occur in the aftermath of a number of different traumas. Some people, like Bill, suffer from PTSD because they have been victims of violent crime. Others have witnessed violence in the home, at school, or in the streets. Yet other people, like Rayetta, live with the symptoms of post-traumatic stress disorder because they experienced sexual, emotional, or physical abuse as young children. Disasters, such as the fire that destroyed Karen's apartment, can also cause those who endure or witness them to have PTSD symptoms long afterward.

Mental-health professionals who treat PTSD have discovered that even the stress of living with a person, such as a combat veteran or an incest victim, whose PTSD is untreated and long-term can produce PTSD in family members.

To his drinking buddies, Carlos's dad seems like a happy-go-lucky kind of person. Sure he changes jobs frequently and he moves his family from place to place every few months, but he's always smiling and ready with a new joke when he sits down to have a beer at the VFW. Carlos, however, has seen another side of his father entirely. When people cut in front of him in traffic, he swears, chases after them, and tries to ram them with his pickup truck. He changes jobs so often because he can't take orders from anybody. The family moves, sometimes before they've unpacked from the last time, because Carlos's father doesn't like to get close to people. The houses they rent must always have basements because he says it makes him feel safer.

Even though his father never talks about Vietnam, Carlos knows that his dad's strange ways have to do with the war. Why else would he have barricaded the whole family in the house last Fourth of July, waiting in the basement for the firecrackers to stop popping? Why else would he sleep with three guns under his bed? One night, Carlos's dad awoke in the middle of a dream, started screaming "Incoming!" and shoved the family down the basement steps. Carlos's little sister fell and broke her arm, but his dad wouldn't let them out to take her to the doctor for hours. Carlos can still hear her screams in his mind.

Carlos has never been near combat, but he's always jumpy and ready for something bad to happen with a split-second's notice. He has a hard time relaxing during the day and going to sleep at night. Lately he feels safer sleeping with a baseball bat beside the bed and a sharp knife under his pillow. Once in a while he even dreams that *he* is in the jungle fighting the North Vietnamese. Although he didn't experience the Vietnam War, Carlos has experienced life with a combat veteran who brought the war home with him. Now that war is a part of Carlos's daily life.

PTSD—A New Name for an Old Problem

Traumatic events are nothing new. Mass tragedies such as wars and natural disasters have been recorded since the beginning of history. For hundreds of years people have known that extremely stressful occasions such as these can often cause people to react in disturbing ways for months and sometimes years after the trauma is over. The ancient Greeks wrote about the same symptoms that Bill, Rayetta, Karen, and Carlos and his father experience. British writer Samuel Pepys detailed his emotional anguish after the London Fire of 1666 with the vivid words that survivors of plane crashes, floods, and fires echo in our time.

More recently, in the mid-1800s, writers Stephen Crane and Walt Whitman recorded the stunning impact the horrors of the Civil War had on the men who fought it. Now some scholars believe that the severely depressed Whitman, who had served as a medic in the Civil War, suffered from PTSD throughout his lifetime as a result of his war experiences.

Shortly before the turn of the century, Sigmund Freud, often called the father of modern psychiatry, talked with women clients who said they had been the victims of incest or other sexual molestation as children. He believed the emotional difficulties these women experienced were a reaction to their childhood traumas. Freud, giving in to pressure from fellow analysts who denied that incest and molestation of children could happen in proper Victorian society, later reversed his position about trauma and its after-effects. These women were *hysterical,* Freud said. The symptoms they experienced sprang from their imaginations and fantasies. He called the cluster of symptoms he saw displayed in these adult clients *neurosis.*

Today mental-health professionals know that incest *does* occur with shocking frequency and that Freud's first theory was in all probability correct—many of his female clients *were* reacting to a very real trauma that had occurred in childhood, not some imaginary conflict. After Freud revised his theory, however, the idea that people who acted differently after experiencing severe emotional shocks were somehow abnormal or mentally ill persisted for years. Psychologists and psychiatrists said that it wasn't the trauma that caused these people to have a difficult time in their lives; instead, it was some character defect or weakness inside of them making them react so strongly for years after a crisis had passed. Sometimes these professionals accused trauma victims of exaggerating or imagining the traumatic experience. For many years, mental-health workers continued to label people who suffered from what we now call PTSD as neurotic and, in some cases, blamed their patients for their difficulties in coping with daily life.

War is one of the most shockingly painful experiences human beings can endure, so it is not surprising that much of what we know about post-traumatic stress disorder today comes from research sponsored by the military to uncover the reasons why soldiers break down emotionally in battle and to find ways to keep them at peak fighting efficiency. When military leaders noticed that many soldiers seemed to fall apart emotionally under the pressure of battle during World War I, they followed the teachings of Sigmund Freud and termed what they saw in their troops *war neurosis*. Some soldiers were emotionally weaker than others and simply couldn't take the stress of war, they decided.

As the fighting continued on a scale never witnessed or experienced by human beings before, it became clear that some outside factor had to be causing the emotional damage these soldiers suffered. Military leaders came to suspect that the noise of the long artillery bombardments common in World War I caused physical brain damage to some soldiers. They called the condition *shell shock*. Because there was no known cure for shell shock, many veterans who were diagnosed with it were sent to government hospitals after the war ended and lived there without treatment until they died years later from old age.

During World War II, the number of military personnel experiencing emotional breakdowns increased 300 percent over those in World War I. A third of those breakdowns were so severe that the people who suffered them were discharged from the military. At one time during World War II, the number of men released from the service for what was now called *acute combat reaction* or *battle fatigue* by military psychologists nearly equaled the number of men being drafted at the time. In fact, almost a quarter of those evacuated from areas where conflict was taking place were removed for severe emotional problems that affected their ability to fight rather than for physical war wounds.

Despite the fact that an estimated one million American troops were severely emotionally scarred by World War II, military researchers remained uncertain about exactly what was wrong with them and often blamed character weakness for their difficulties, which included nightmares about battle, anxiety, depression, the inability to get along with people, and violent outbursts. A few years after World War II ended, men who had fought bravely and had seemed perfectly fine when they had been discharged began showing up at Veterans Administration hospitals with the same symptoms as those men who had been discharged for acute combat reaction during the war. During this same period researchers studying the survivors of Nazi concentration camps also began to notice that most of the people they were observing shared the same problems of combat veterans.

By that time the Korean War had begun to heat up. By now psychologists were starting to suspect that the trauma of war itself must play a much greater role in causing soldiers to have mental breakdowns than so-called character weaknesses the men carried with them into battle. They began treating emotionally distressed soldiers near the battlefield instead of shipping them home and discharging them. The plan worked. After short-term treatment, most of the men were able to resume their combat duties. Only 6 percent of the men evacuated from Korea were sent home for emotional rather than physical injuries.

Confident that they had solved the problem of acute combat reaction, military psychologists were now certain that the next war would bring an even lower rate of emotional breakdown among the troops. Their experience in Korea led them to advise limiting the time soldiers spent in the war zone to 12 months (13 months in the case of the Marines). Individuals would be removed from combat before they had a chance to develop battle fatigue. At the beginning of the Vietnam War, the strategy seemed to work; the number of military people suffering from psychological breakdown on the battlefield dropped dramatically to 12 out of every 1,000 soldiers.

In the 1970s, though, as the Vietnam War wound down and finally ended, it became obvious that soldiers serving in Vietnam had suffered emotionally to an even greater extent than had any troops fighting in previous wars. Well after the Vietnam War had ended, Veterans Administration hospitals were overwhelmed by the number of men showing up with the same symptoms researchers had noticed in World War II veterans. They suspected that many more Vietnam veterans were not asking for help. They were right. Eventually the 1988 National Vietnam Veterans Readjustment Study, conducted by the Research Triangle, would find that fully one-third of the troops who served in the Vietnam War have suffered from post-traumatic stress disorder at some time in their lives.

As Veterans Administration counselors began to talk with these Vietnam veterans in an attempt to help them readjust to civilian life after the war, they encountered the same symptoms over and over again—nightmares about battle, anxiety, depression, the inability to get along with people, and violent outbursts. Eventually, they realized without a doubt that the veterans' current difficulties had very little to do with previous emotional troubles. The life-threatening, bloody trauma of war was responsible for their current problems. Psychologists began to call the collection of symptoms they saw so often in the V.A. hospitals and at Vet Centers *post-traumatic stress disorder,* a name that finally removed all blame from war's emotional casualties, placing the focus on the trauma where it belonged.

At about the same time that psychologists were observing the Vietnam veterans and trying to find a way to treat them, many other researchers began studying survivors of plane crashes, natural disasters, and terrorist acts. They noticed that quite a few of these people struggled with the same problems that the veterans did. They began to realize that in the past, people who had displayed the symptoms of post-traumatic stress disorder had often been given the wrong diagnosis, sometimes being labeled depressed, anti-social or even schizophrenic. Their therapists had completely ignored the trauma that had triggered their problems. In 1980, in an attempt to correct this situation, the American Psychiatric Association included post-traumatic stress disorder in its *Diagnostic and Statistical Manual III,* the standard handbook used to diagnose emotional disorders.

Much more research has been done on PTSD in the years that have followed. It is now known that a large number of people in our society suffer from the collection of symptoms that makes up PTSD—from ambulance drivers and battered women to flood victims and children of alcoholics. Many of these people don't seek professional treatment for their lingering problems because they don't know that they have PTSD or that they can be helped. According to information from the American Psychiatric Association, as many as 1 in 10 people in the general population have post-traumatic stress disorder severe enough to meet the standards set forth in their *Diagnostical and Statistical Manual.* Many more people experience difficulty with at least a few of the symptoms after a trauma.

The rates of PTSD are much higher within *at-risk groups,* groups of people that have a greater chance of experiencing trauma than in the general population. For example, researchers Dean Kilpatrick and Heidi Resnick have found that crime victims have a 19 to 75 percent chance of experiencing PTSD, depending on the type of crime they experienced. People who live in areas with high crime rates are a high risk PTSD group. Rape victims seem to have the highest rates of PTSD. Not surprisingly, more women than men appear to suffer from PTSD.

As violence in our society escalates, many more people are experiencing traumas than ever before. According to psychologist Raymond B. Flannery, author of *Post-Traumatic Stress Disorder: The Victim's Guide to Healing and Recovery*, 14 percent of all Americans are victims of crime each year, 25 percent of all women have been battered, 25 percent of all women have been sexually abused, and 20 percent of all men have been sexually abused. One hundred children die each month from abuse and neglect, one child is raped every 45 minutes, and one teenager commits suicide every 49 minutes. Writes Flannery, "Such traumatic events are frightening and depressingly common. The exact extent of such violence is difficult to determine because reporting methods differ from one policing or health care agency to another, and because many victims do not report these events at all. A recent and reliable study, however, has estimated that as many as two and one-half to possibly five million Americans may be suffering from the harmful effects of PTSD." The chance that you or someone you love will experience PTSD within your lifetime is high and growing higher by the moment.

Stress or Trauma?

Think about the last time you were nervous. How did your body feel? Did your stomach feel twisted, like it was tied in a knot? Were the palms of your hands sweaty? Did your muscles tense? Were you shaky? Now remember what it was that caused you to feel that way. The event that made you feel so anxious and uncomfortable is called a *stress-producing event* or a *stressor.*

All of us face some stressors in our daily lives—getting a bad grade on a test, being teased by our friends in front of someone we're trying to impress, getting lost in an unfamiliar city. Most of the time we feel a little discomfort when we experience these stressful periods, but once we have come out on the other side in one piece, we put the event and uneasy feelings behind us.

Occasionally, though, the stressors in our lives can be so intense and emotionally shocking that they leave lasting psychological scars. Stressors of this degree are called *traumas.* Before a person can be diagnosed as having developed PTSD, he or she must experience a trauma. Some mental-health professionals call PTSD a natural reaction to an unnatural situation. (In Chapter Two we'll explore how the symptoms of PTSD actually help a person survive during a traumatic crisis. It is only *after* the trauma passes that they become harmful to those who suffer them.)

Take a few minutes to read through the following situations. On a separate piece of paper, rank them in your opinion from least to most emotionally stressful (one would be the least stressful and six the most). Now mark the ones you feel would be stressors for you with an *S* and those you consider might be traumas with a *T.*

1. While your family is away on vacation, someone breaks into your home and vandalizes it. No one is hurt, but the walls in your room are spray painted with obscenities and all your clothing is slashed to shreds.

2. As your mother stops the car at an intersection on the way to school one morning, you see another car make a left turn and hit one of your classmates. Your friend is caught beneath the speeding car and dragged for quite a distance, leaving a trail of blood on the pavement. Later that day you learn your friend has died.

3. Your favorite uncle asks if you would like to fly across the country and spend a month with him during your vacation—he'll buy the tickets. Your parents agree. Once you're there, he starts acting strangely. He demands to see you naked and touches you sexually. When you threaten to tell, he threatens to tell your parents *you* were the one who seduced him.

4. Your grandmother, who is 84 and who you know has a history of heart trouble, dies suddenly in her sleep.

5. When your soccer coach is upset at team members, he swears at them. Sometimes it seems as though he singles you out for verbal abuse. One day he gets so angry with you he twists your arm behind your back and says he'll break it if you don't shape up.

6. You're eating dinner with your family when a gunman comes into the fast-food restaurant and orders everyone to lie on the floor. He threatens to kill everyone and fires several rounds of ammunition into the ceiling. After holding you hostage for several hours, he releases you and your family unharmed.

There are no right or wrong answers to the quiz above. Every situation described has the potential to be traumatic. How you respond to the questions depends on your individual values and the events which have occurred in your life until this moment. For example, if your grandmother was one of the most significant people in your life, her death would mean something different to you than if you hardly knew her because you'd been raised halfway across the country from where she had lived. Since each individual is different and holds different values, an event can be very traumatic to some people yet cause little lasting emotional harm to others. Other reasons why some people have PTSD and some do not after a trauma will be covered later.

The Aftermath of Trauma

After Bill was mugged, he shoved his fear inside and kept walking the same route home at night from his friend's house. Even though he had nightmares about the beating, he tried to ignore them and pretend that everything was fine. Nonetheless, he still feels angry much of the time and doesn't trust other people. Rayetta experienced panic attacks and started having flashbacks as the memories of having been sexually molested as a child began to slowly come back to her conscious mind. She feels like she has no control over her emotions anymore and wants to hide from them. Karen went numb and has lost her interest in life. She spends her time obsessing about what she will do if there is another fire. When Carlos's father hears a loud noise or has a bad dream, he thinks he's back in Vietnam. His misguided attempts to protect his family from death hurt them. Carlos can't relax; he's always expecting something terrible to happen.

Because they suffer from post-traumatic stress disorder, Bill, Rayetta, Karen, Carlos, and his father don't understand and often can't sort out the wild mix of their feelings, thoughts, and actions, but the professionals who study and treat PTSD separate the symptoms of the disorder into three distinct categories. These categories are:

Intrusive Symptoms—Things that cause a person to involuntarily reexperience the traumatic event.

Avoidance Symptoms—The avoidance of anything that will trigger memories of the trauma, such as things associated with the trauma and even certain feelings.

Increased Arousal Symptoms—Signs that the person is both emotionally and physically in a state of constant readiness in case the trauma happens again.

Intrusive Symptoms

Intrusive symptoms are the brain's way of forcing a person who has experienced a trauma to work through the event that has turned his or her world upside down. Nightmares of the sort that Bill, Rayetta, Carlos, and his father have had are considered intrusive symptoms of PTSD. These dreams, during which the traumatic event seems to demand attention, tend to repeat themselves over and over again, returning in cycles. They may disappear completely for a few nights or a few months, and then suddenly the same dream may take place several times in one night.

Often these dreams are so intense that they cause a physical reaction, like the one Rayetta had when she became sick to her stomach. When people are in the middle of an intrusive traumatic dream, they may yell, thrash about, or even attack another person as they act out the nightmare in their sleep. Some wives of Vietnam veterans report that they have been traumatically awakened by their husbands' hands around their necks—the men thought their spouses were North Vietnamese and were trying to kill them. The veterans' actions were completely out of their control. It is no wonder that people who have PTSD have a difficult time falling asleep—and going back to sleep—after these dreams occur, or that people who live with PTSD sufferers may begin experiencing the symptoms of PTSD themselves.

During their waking hours, people with PTSD are often haunted by unwanted memories of the past trauma, like Karen, who constantly planned and revised her escape route in case there was another fire in her house. The surviving driver in a fatal car crash may replay the accident over and over again in his or her mind, trying to figure out what could have been done differently. A rescue worker may be plagued with images of dead bodies that intrude on his or her thoughts without warning. No matter how hard a person with PTSD tries to remove these thoughts from his or her consciousness, they always seem to come back. Often they are accompanied by an overwhelming surge of anger, fear, or guilt. Sometimes that guilt is about surviving the trauma when other people have died because of it.

At times these emotions can well up without the memory. In Rayetta's case, fear, disgust, and anger were triggered by Paul's flirting. She wasn't afraid, disgusted, or angry at *him*—she was reexperiencing what she had felt when her mother's boyfriend had molested her years before, an event she couldn't clearly remember. The emotional distress that comes from triggers like Paul's flirting or the Fourth of July fireworks that sent Carlos's dad into a panic are another symptom of PTSD. These triggers can be anything that represents or reminds the person of the trauma. A noise, a smell, a word, even the anniversary date of the emotionally shocking event is enough to unleash another uncontrollable storm of emotions.

Sometimes the waking memories and triggered emotions of PTSD are so strong that the person who has them *disassociates* and has *flashbacks*. Although the person doesn't lose consciousness, he or she loses touch with reality, believing the traumatic event is happening all over again. Many times they act on that belief. When Carlos and his family were herded down the basement stairs, his dad really did think there was an incoming artillery attack and that if he didn't save them, his wife and children would be killed. His flashback lasted for hours. Sometimes, however, flashbacks come and go very rapidly. Soon after Rayetta ran from the arcade, her flashback ended leaving her feeling ashamed and confused.

Avoidance Symptoms
Because thinking about what has happened to them is so painful and intrusive symptoms are so distressing, people

with PTSD usually attempt to avoid all reminders of the traumatic event. Like Bill, they may refuse to talk about it, or, like Rayetta, their subconscious minds suppress the trauma or parts of it from memory. When the latter happens it is called *psychogenic* or *stress-induced amnesia.* Many people with PTSD avoid getting professional help because they are terrified that talking with a therapist will set off another round of intrusive symptoms in the form of uncontrollable thoughts, nightmares, and flashbacks.

In time, those who suffer from post-traumatic stress disorder learn to manage their lives so that they can bypass activities and situations that will cause the old feelings that surround the traumatic event to well up. A Vietnam combat veteran may avoid eating in Vietnamese restaurants so he doesn't ever have to see people who will remotely remind him of his former enemy. A woman who has been a rape victim might completely avoid men. Someone who has been involved in or witnessed a gruesome automobile accident may avoid driving or even riding in cars. One of the reasons Carlos's dad has great difficulty holding a job is that he hates being told what to do by a boss. It reminds him too much of the times he had to take orders during the war.

Quite often PTSD sufferers stop participating in activities that used to give them pleasure, such as sports, hobbies, and work. They may withdraw from the world as Karen did, keeping to themselves and pulling away from old friends. At times, even leaving the house or getting out of bed in the morning takes a great deal of effort. Many people with PTSD find themselves unable to plan for the future. They are too busy surviving in the present, and they walk around convinced that at any moment another trauma could devastate their lives again. For this reason they often have difficulty in school, at work, and in their home lives. It is no wonder that before post-traumatic stress disorder was recognized and written about, many mental-health professionals mistook the problem for depression.

Just as the body tends to shut down or go into shock when it has been severely injured, the mind responds to extreme emotional injury by what is called *psychic numbing*. In the aftermath of severe trauma, many people shut down so far emotionally that they say they can't feel a thing. A formerly loving spouse or parent may become cold and distant as all emotions are turned off, even the positive ones like love and joy. They may feel cut off from other people. This feeling of being cut off is called *alienation*.

Increased Arousal

Remember the last time someone played a joke on you by creeping up silently behind you and then yelling "Boo!" in your ear when you least expected it. If you're like most of us, you probably jumped involuntarily and had to fight the urge to smack the person. You probably felt embarrassed, too, when the person who tricked you and everyone else began laughing at your response. Now imagine going through life always so on edge that any surprising noise or sudden move, even a minor one, leaves you feeling scared to death and then angry. How would you feel if this happened several times a day? That's what PTSD can do to people who suffer from it. They have what is known as an *exaggerated startle response;* the edgy, jumpy feeling that causes it is called *hyperarousal.*

Hyperarousal is the body's way of making certain a person is physically and emotionally ready to fight or flee a crisis, should one come along. When Rayetta froze in her seat in response to Paul's flirting, she was in a state of hyperarousal. In addition to an exaggerated startle response, people with symptoms of hyperarousal often have sleep difficulties—they either have trouble falling asleep or may be light sleepers who awaken several times a night because the slightest sound awakens them. Often they prepare ahead, just in case something bad happens. Carlos's dad sleeps with guns under his bed, more guns than he would possibly need to stop an intruder. Carlos, who has developed PTSD from living with his father, feels like he needs the extra protection of a baseball bat beside his bed before he can let his guard down enough to sleep.

Because they are so constantly geared up for disaster, people with hyperarousal symptoms often have trouble concentrating on daily tasks and find it hard to remember things. Their minds are elsewhere. Even though Bill denied that being mugged by gang members had affected him very much, not only was he unable to sleep, he started failing his classes in school. This happened partly because he was too tired to focus, but also because he was too busy weighing the possibility of another gang attack to have any energy left for his studies.

Some people in states of hyperarousal are *hypervigilant*—they are constantly observing everything around them, looking for trouble like Bill did in the classroom. People with PTSD often feel distress when others sit behind them in a movie theater or restaurant. Most of the time they prefer a seat where they can keep an eye on everyone and have a clear path to the nearest exit. They want their environment always to be under their control. Sometimes this concern extends to the safety of friends and family members. The person who has PTSD may demand to know where loved ones are all of the time and may forbid them from going places because he or she fears they will be harmed or killed.

When Rayetta vomited after her dreams and when she started hyperventilating at the arcade, she was experiencing another PTSD symptom, called *physiological reactivity,* a physical response to a trigger that is a reminder of the trauma. Some of the other ways people with PTSD may respond to a trauma trigger are by trembling, breaking out in a sweat, feeling dizzy, or even by fainting.

Because they are tense and ready for action so much of the time, many people with post-traumatic stress disorder are often irritable and may lash out in anger at other people without knowing why. Their anger either isn't related to what is currently happening in their lives or it is out of proportion to it. Carlos's father becomes enraged by other drivers. Sometimes it is all he can do to keep himself from attacking them. His anger stems from the tension he always feels, tension that is ready to boil over with very little provocation.

Associated Features

In addition to the three categories of symptoms directly related to PTSD, trauma victims often have problems with what psychologists call *associated features,* difficulties that aren't actually caused by the trauma but that often occur after an emotionally shocking experience. These associated features aren't a part of post-traumatic stress disorder, and they cause trauma victims to suffer to an even greater degree than they would from PTSD alone.

Quite frequently people who have PTSD use alcohol or drugs in an effort to "self-medicate" their symptoms. When they are drunk or drugged they may sleep more easily, and for a short time they feel in control of their lives even though in reality they are less in control when they are under the influence of mood-altering substances.

Other people with PTSD show poor control over their impulses. A person with poor impulse control might disappear for days at a time with no explanation or commit a crime without ever thinking of the consequences. Carlos's dad moves his family whenever he gets the urge, without stopping to think about how those frequent moves are affecting his children. It isn't that he doesn't care about his family—his actions are as out of his control as his startle response, flashbacks, or his days spent in the combat zone.

The symptoms of PTSD can vary considerably from person to person. According to the current American Psychiatric Association guidelines that psychologists and psychiatrists use to diagnose PTSD, a person must be experiencing at least one intrusive symptom, three or more avoidance symptoms, and two or more symptoms of increased arousal before they are said to have PTSD. Even though a traumatized individual may have some or all of these symptoms, his or her problems must continue for more than a month before mental-health professionals will diagnose that person as having post-traumatic stress disorder.

Many mental-health workers diagnose trauma victims who experience five or fewer symptoms and experience them for more than a month as having *partial PTSD*. They believe that even people with partial PTSD have been emotionally wounded and go through a tremendous amount of emotional pain. Just as people diagnosed with full-blown PTSD, they, too, can often greatly improve their lives by seeking counseling in order to heal from the traumatic event.

2

Prisoners of the Past: Why PTSD Occurs

In the last chapter you remembered a time you felt stress. Now take a minute to remember a time when you felt really scared. Maybe you were riding on a roller coaster or another amusement park ride that suddenly stopped being fun and caused you to panic. Or perhaps you were alone at home after dark watching a horror video when a strange noise from outside frightened you out of your wits. Maybe you woke up from a nightmare that seemed so real and was so horrible that you needed a few minutes to figure out that you were safe in your own bed. Your memory might be of a time when you were in a car wreck or another dangerous situation that made you fear for your life. On a separate sheet of paper briefly describe how your body felt and the thoughts and emotions that raced through your mind.

Chances are some of the words you used in this description are the same as those you thought of when you remembered the stressful situation. It could be that the palms of your hands began to sweat and that your heart pounded so loudly you could hear it. Maybe you felt dizzy and sick to your stomach. Your thoughts might have been scattered and confused so that it was difficult for you to know what to do next. As we discussed earlier, stress causes both physical and emotional reactions in people.

Extreme stress or trauma takes those automatic and very normal reactions a few steps further. In all probability, your description of how you felt when you were terrified includes some new items in addition to the old ones. Perhaps you became so disoriented that you felt like you were going to fall apart or maybe you were so calm, cool, and collected that your actions seemed mechanical, almost as though you were a robot. Your vision and hearing might have either become worse or seemed much sharper than usual. The blood may have drained from your face, making your skin pale. It could be that you felt weak and passed out. Or maybe you felt stronger and were able to do things you didn't know you could do before, like running faster than you'd ever run in your life or lifting something very heavy that you couldn't under normal circumstances.

These reactions of mind and body are all normal responses to an extreme crisis. They are automatic ways of coping with traumatic stress. They may keep us alive or relatively safe during a trauma, but they form the basis for the symptoms of PTSD, which may continue long after the crisis or occur much later and cause us a great deal of emotional suffering.

When Bill heard the footsteps behind him the night he was mugged, the tiny hairs on the back of his neck seemed to stand up in response to the danger he sensed and the fear he felt. He became extremely alert, his ears sharp for even the slightest sound and his vision especially keen as he scanned the sidewalk ahead of him for an escape route.

Seconds earlier he'd been thinking about the math test he had to take the next day and how to get an advance on his allowance from his dad so that he could buy a new CD he wanted. Now those thoughts vanished in an instant as his mind began operating with the speed of a powerful computer, coming up with plans about what to do if the people following him tried to hurt him.

Once the gang members charged forward, a surge of energy ran through Bill's body and he began to flee faster than he had ever remembered running. Unfortunately, he wasn't fast enough. He certainly wasn't a coward, and in the past he'd assumed he'd fight if anybody ever attacked him, but Bill hadn't counted on taking on five people at once.

Knocked to the ground, Bill tried to reason with his attackers. He was shocked at how calm his voice sounded. It was as if he wasn't doing the talking—the words were just coming out on their own. Once the gang members began smashing his face and throwing punches to his stomach, Bill shut down. Even though the beating hurt, he didn't feel that much, not even when one of the boys pulled a knife and cut him on the arm. It was like the Novocain shots they gave at the dentist's office. He was numb to the point that it seemed as though he was watching a movie and somebody else was taking the punches. The fear he'd felt earlier left him completely. In its place was a cold determination to endure.

After the gang members left with Bill's money, he was so bruised and battered that he could hardly walk. Somehow he managed to drag himself home. He didn't know quite how. By all rights, he shouldn't have even been able to walk. As soon as he made it through the front door of his house, though, he collapsed in a heap on the living room floor, exhausted. It wasn't until he was lying on the examining table at the hospital emergency room and the doctor was sewing up his cut that the pain really began to hit him. The fear came back, too. Even though the danger had passed, his hands shook, and he thought he was going to pass out.

The Trauma Response

The way Bill responded to the attack on him by gang members is a fairly typical pattern of human reaction to trauma. When he first sensed possible danger, Bill's adrenal glands began manufacturing epinephrine, cortisol, and norepinephrine, chemical substances that prepare the body to deal with the danger at hand by either defending itself or running away. The epinephrine and cortisol sent a message to Bill's brain, speeding his heart rate and helping to regulate his breathing and muscles so that he would be ready for anything. In addition, the pupils of his eyes immediately dilated, helping him to see better. This physical reaction is known as the *fight or flight response,* and is the way nature has provided for human beings to survive in a dangerous world when there is no time for deliberate thought. Some people call these physical sensations an adrenaline rush.

Cortisol is what gives people in crisis seemingly superhuman strength to do what is necessary, whether it is to lift an automobile from someone who is trapped beneath it or to swim with the speed of an Olympic gold medalist in order to save a drowning child. Cortisol keeps soldiers fighting for days with no sleep. These bursts of energy happen when cortisol signals *glucose,* or blood sugar, to be released into the bloodstream. Once the crisis has passed and blood-sugar levels have dropped, the person who just went through a crisis usually feels drained of strength and exhausted.

An important part of the fight or flight response is *hyperarousal,* a symptom discussed earlier. A person facing danger is acutely sensitive to everything in his or her surroundings. Movements, sounds, smells, sights, and physical sensations that would otherwise go unnoticed, now all receive immediate attention because they can help the person going through a traumatic event to stay alive. Norepinephrine, which is released by the adrenal glands and travels to the brain, causes alertness and quickens the mind so that people in danger can think fast and come up with solutions about how to get out of danger.

Bill's hyperalertness was much like what a soldier in a battle area experiences. If a combat soldier doesn't pay close attention to every environmental cue and clue about what might be going on around him, no matter how small, he could walk into an ambush and be killed. Animals as well as human beings are gifted with the ability to become hyperalert. When they sense the presence of a predator or enemy, their senses also become more acute.

When it is impossible to fight or to run away, or when a person in the midst of trauma has been physically injured, hyperalertness *isn't* a help. In these circumstances it can cut down that person's chances for survival. If you broke your leg in an automobile accident on a rural road in the wintertime and were the only one in the car who remained conscious, you would need to take immediate action to save yourself and the other accident victims. Being sharply aware of the pain from your broken leg would make it nearly impossible for you to drag the other people from the vehicles—even if there was a possibility the cars would catch on fire. By the same token, you'd have a terrible time making your way to the nearest farmhouse if your hyper-alertness made you extrasensitive to the cold.

Nature has planned for that possibility by giving human beings yet another automatic way of responding to trauma—shutting down. Sometimes people in the middle of an extreme crisis find themselves experiencing tunnel vision, a condition during which they can only see straight ahead, or they may temporarily lose their hearing. Often they don't feel pain, either from their injuries or from the strain of physical exertion. Their bodies protect them from feeling too much by producing high levels of *endorphins,* natural chemicals made by the brain that resemble painkilling drugs, or *opiates.* When Bill was cut and beaten, he experienced what psychologists and doctors call *stress induced analgesia.* He didn't feel much pain because his brain had released endorphins. This lack of feeling helped him because it allowed him to roll with the punches and manage to make his way home after his attackers left.

Emotions often only serve to get in the way during extreme trauma. Being scared to death or so mad you couldn't see straight would mean you might make a mistake that could cost you your life. During a traumatic event, feelings are a luxury with a high price. People in trauma *do* experience some degree of terror, grief, confusion, anger, and self-blame, but even though those powerful feelings exist, there is no time to feel and work through them.

For this reason, the body makes certain that emotions, as well as physical sensations, are shut down during times of severe stress. For example, even though Carlos's father saw many of his friends killed during the war, he didn't have time to feel sad when it happened. If in the middle of an artillery barrage, he had stopped to grieve or to feel scared that he might meet the same end as his friends, he would have been killed in the fighting, too. Instead, his body released endorphins that helped to push those emotions deep down inside of him so that he could do a good job as a soldier. This automatic survival technique is called *emotional numbing.*

The emotional shutdown may be so complete that the person who experiences it actually *disassociates.* Their mental and emotional awareness splits off from their body and sense of self. Like Bill, they may feel like they are watching a movie of something happening to somebody else. What is going on around them seems unreal, and they remain emotionally detached from it. When Rayetta was sexually abused as a child by her mother's boyfriend, her mind went somewhere else. Usually she thought about being at school or in the playground at the neighborhood park. Disassociation kept her from feeling physical and emotional pain at a time when she couldn't do anything to stop the abuse from happening. Often people who remain unusually calm in crisis, those who seem not to be affected at all by the chaos around them, have disassociated.

After the Trauma

Once a crisis has passed, whether it was a battle, a tornado, or a mugging, many people find that their emotional and physical balance is slowly restored as their levels of cortisol, norepinephrine, and endorphins return to normal. For them, time seems to heal the emotional wounds the trauma has inflicted. Other people who appeared extremely calm after an intense emotional shock, and who may even deny the crisis has affected them in the least bit, haven't really calmed down. Instead, they continue to disassociate or detach themselves from what has happened and go on repressing their feelings. These people are the most likely to develop *delayed onset post-traumatic stress disorder,* like Rayetta. Their symptoms, such as nightmares and flash-backs, often remain hidden, not appearing until months or years later.

Emotional and physical reactions to crisis often continue for weeks or months, especially when the trauma was a severe one and the victim received little or no help in dealing with the strong emotions that surrounded the event. Even when help is available, the process of recovering from an emotional shock often takes time. All of the feelings that the body blocked out during the traumatic event must be dealt with one by one. The struggle of trauma survivors to make sense of what has happened is often not an easy one.

Traumas attack our basic beliefs about who we are, the nature of others, and how the world works. After we go through a severe emotional shock we may find ourselves asking questions like: Who can I trust? What do I believe? Why did this thing happen to me? Sometimes the answers to those questions are negative ones. Like Bill, we may decide we can't trust anybody because we don't know who will hurt us. Carlos has learned that he can't trust his own father not to hurt him. Rayetta doesn't only mistrust boys; she mistrusts her own blossoming sexual feelings. When we experience random violence, as Bill did, or a disaster, such as Karen's, the world no longer seems a safe place in which to live. We can't predict when trauma will happen to us again. For a time, at least, we are left feeling powerless and helpless. The feeling that what happens to us is beyond our control causes us to lose our self-esteem.

Often other people—even those who have also under-gone the crisis—expect trauma victims to "snap out of it" and get back to normal soon after the event has happened. Victims of extreme crisis may be told to put the emotional shock behind them right away.

For Karen's mother the apartment fire was unpleasant and a major inconvenience, but it wasn't a traumatic stress. The experience of losing everything and barely escaping being burned *was* very traumatic to Karen. She felt guilty that she had survived the fire when her cat had died what she assumed to be a painful death. When Karen's mom told her to stop worrying, that her cat was just a pet not a person, Karen stopped talking about her feelings. As the weeks progressed and Karen's mom continued advising her daughter that she should feel grateful and go on with her life, Karen spent more and more time in her room, saying that she was studying. It seemed to her that nobody understood her feelings. Maybe it was wrong to even have those feelings. Because Karen had no one she trusted to talk with about the trauma, she was forced to make sense of it on her own, a job that was too big for her.

According to the Social Work Subcommittee of the Society for Traumatic Stress Studies, the aftermath of trauma affects several areas of people's lives—their bodies, emotions, behavior, ability to think and get along with others, and how they relate to the world around them. Even when these aftereffects are relatively short-lived, they make adjusting to everyday life after a crisis a difficult task for anyone—even people who don't go on to develop PTSD.

Biological Effects

As mentioned earlier, people who have recently experienced a traumatic event often have difficulty sleeping. They may also suffer from extreme tiredness. When the physical effects of trauma continue over a long period of time, people who experience prolonged hyperalertness and anxiety may start to suffer from stress-related illnesses such as high blood pressure, ulcers, and muscle aches and pains.

Emotional Effects

Some trauma victims remain emotionally numb after the danger has passed, their feelings about what has happened deeply suppressed. For others, the emotions of fear, anger, shame, anxiety, and sadness, which were shut out from consciousness during the traumatic event, start to surface in the days or weeks afterward, causing angry outbursts and sudden crying spells that may seem to happen for no reason. People who have gone through severe crisis also may begin to experience *survivor guilt.* Like Karen, they feel bad about escaping injury or death when others weren't so fortunate.

Sometimes the sense of helplessness that survivors experienced during the traumatic event is carried forward, so that adult trauma survivors may feel and sometimes act like little children. (Children who are victims sometimes start to act much younger than their age.) When this happens, it is called *regression*. Soon after experiencing a trauma, people are more vulnerable to other stresses in their lives, too, such as those that normally occur in the family or at work. Their reactions after the trauma can be stressful in and of themselves.

Mental Effects

After a traumatic event has passed, those who have lived through it often feel disoriented or confused. The world simply doesn't seem to make sense anymore. It may be difficult for them to think about or to concentrate on much of anything besides the trauma or on trying to shove the trauma from their minds. Short-term memory often suffers as well.

The intrusive symptoms discussed in Chapter One can appear soon after the crisis is over. Often people who have experienced a trauma have flashbacks or they run through the events that recently occurred over and over again in their minds, obsessing about what might have happened if only they'd done something differently. At night, terrifying nightmares may replace the flashbacks as their minds work overtime to find the meaning in the terrible thing that has happened.

Behavioral Effects

Sometimes people who undergo severe trauma are so overcome by emotions that they begin acting out in self-destructive ways. Children who have been sexually molested may practice *self-mutilation,* or cut themselves. A combat veteran might take up a high-risk sport, such as hang gliding, throwing safety precautions to the wind in an almost suicidal move. Alcohol and drug abuse, as well as eating disorders, are other behavioral side-effects of trauma that can wreak havoc on a survivor's life.

Interpersonal Effects

Frequently trauma victims have a difficult time relating to other people after the crisis. Some trauma victims become very passive around others because they have learned to be helpless from an experience in which their fate was out of their control. If the trauma has involved being victimized by another person, the target of the assault may avoid both emotional and physical closeness with others, including family members. That person simply doesn't trust anyone enough to let them get close. Many times this self-imposed distancing and coldness in relationships alternates with what psychologists call *enmeshment,* relationships that are so close and constricting that the people involved in them don't know where one individual leaves off and the other begins.

Often people who have been traumatized by something another person has done to them react by putting themselves in other situations in which they will experience a similar trauma. For example, a woman who was molested as a child might date sexually aggressive men who resemble the man who sexually assaulted her. According to psychologists, this *revictimization* is a subconscious attempt to work through the trauma. It is almost as if the person, by repeating the trauma over and over again, is trying to get it to turn out right.

The Causes of PTSD

Biology

Recently a number of researchers have begun to study the effects of norepinephrine, the neurotransmitter produced by the adrenal glands as a reaction to stress. They are also studying endorphins and serotonin, neurochemicals released by the brain in large amounts during extreme stress or trauma. They believe that these biochemicals have a long-term effect on trauma victims and that they may either cause or contribute to the symptoms of PTSD months and even years after the severe stress has passed.

Several of these researchers, including Wilson and van der Kolk, believe that brain biochemistry may be permanently changed by trauma. Norepinephrine, which surges through the body during extreme stress and which is responsible for hyperalertness, flashbacks, and nightmares, continues to be manufactured in greater amounts after the trauma has passed than before the trauma occurred. Over time the nerves in the *limbic system,* the part of the brain that controls emotion, are changed so that only a tiny bit of norepinephrine will *kindle* or provoke an intense reaction to something that reminds a trauma victim of the traumatic event. When Carlos's father orders his family into the basement when firecrackers pop, even though he knows it's the Fourth of July, he can't help himself. His actions are driven in part by brain chemistry.

Soon after the brain releases norepinephrine in response to stress, it begins to release endorphins. The combination of these two neurochemicals has been found by researchers to help us learn quickly and permanently. Some researchers believe that trauma victims who develop PTSD have the memories of trauma etched into their brains permanently. At the time of the crisis, this super-learning is helpful because it aids people in taking care of themselves and staying alive. After the trauma, though, it results in obsessive thoughts, and provides the content of flashbacks. A few researchers believe the *neural pathways,* nerve fibers that serve as routes over which the brain's impulses travel, are permanently altered once this super-learning takes place. It becomes easier for information, thoughts, and impulses that have to do with the trauma to travel through the brain than those that have to do with everyday life.

When the brain focuses on the trauma through obsessive thoughts, flashbacks, or dreams, these intrusive symptoms trigger stepped-up endorphin production. High levels of endorphins seem to strengthen numbing avoidance symptoms like denial and detachment that people with PTSD experience. The natural opiate, endorphin, as you will remember, numbs emotional as well as physical pain. According to psychologist Raymond B. Flannery, when endorphin levels drop, people go through what is called *endorphin withdrawal.* Their bodies have come to depend on the neurochemical, and when levels go down, they become restless and agitated.

Some researchers believe that serotonin, another neurochemical always present in our brains, also serves this function. When our brains are manufacturing just the right amounts of serotonin, we are calm and relaxed. Serotonin is depleted by stress, and when our serotonin levels go down, we become irritable, just as we do when our endorphin levels drop. People with low serotonin and endorphin levels are prone to emotional outbursts, a common symptom of PTSD.

Researchers Burges-Watson, Hoffman, and Wilson believe that an imbalance between norepinephrine and endorphins may be responsible for the swings between intrusive and avoidance symptoms that people with PTSD often experience. They think that an increased sensitivity to norepinephrine may be what causes some people, like veterans who become mercenaries, to repeat the trauma. After these repetitions, their endorphin levels rise and they experience a period of relative calm.

Other people with PTSD seem to become addicted to behaviors like gambling, eating, or sex, which increase endorphin levels. Still others mistakenly try to make themselves feel better by using drugs or alcohol. These activities have all been shown to raise endorphin levels. More positive ways of increasing the body's production of endorphins are relaxation exercises and physical exertion. Those trauma victims who don't find a way, either negative or positive, to coax their brains into making more endorphins experience a surge in norepinephrine, just enough to kindle stressful flashback or nightmare. This, in turn, triggers a release of endorphins. When endorphin levels drop, the vicious neurochemical cycle starts all over again.

Patricia Ver Ellen, a professor of psychiatry, and Daniel P. van Kammen, chief of staff at the Veterans Affairs Medical Center in Pittsburgh, Pennsylvania, reviewed nearly a hundred research studies of the biology of PTSD. They concluded that, depending on the type and severity, PTSD may cause permanent changes that actually damage the brain to some extent. The repeated pattern of intrusive symptoms and avoidance symptoms coupled with the neurochemicals that accompany them may cause permanent and ongoing harm to the brain cells of people with chronic PTSD, especially those who don't seek treatment.

Psychology

Although PTSD has a biological basis, brain chemistry isn't the only thing that causes symptoms to occur. Our ability to master the world and make sense of it as well as our ability to form attachments can all be shattered in an instant by trauma. We may question our self-worth and feel that life has no purpose for us. Such events leave us feeling fearful and off-balance. They also leave us with a number of negative emotions, such as grief, anger, shame, guilt, and depression. In addition to having a biological basis, the symptoms of PTSD can be a psychological, subconscious attempt to cope with overwhelming feelings and self-doubts.

According to Mardi J. Horowitz, whose theories about PTSD provided the foundation for the American Psychiatric Association's definition, trauma bombards us with much more external and internal information than we're used to processing, or thinking through. Because this information is so very different from that we are accustomed to dealing with in our daily lives, very little of it fits with how we believe the world should operate, notions we've been developing since we were born.

Some common assumptions that a person might have formed about himself or herself and the way the world works from a very young age might include:

- My home is a safe place.
- Most people can be trusted.
- I'm a strong person, and have control over what happens to me.
- Bad things only happen to other people.
- I have a routine and, most of the time, a good idea about what will happen next.

Take a minute or two to think about the assumptions you have been forming about yourself and about life ever since your birth. Make a brief list. Most of your actions are based on these basic premises that you have just written down. Now imagine how you would feel if suddenly you couldn't believe any of those things anymore. This is how people with PTSD feel, particularly right after the trauma.

Major emotional shocks like car accidents and random violence give us so much new information that just doesn't fit with what we assume to be true that we become overloaded, much like an electrical outlet that has too many appliances plugged into it. Often we can't balance these ideas, feelings, and images with who we are, so we push them out of awareness by denying them and becoming emotionally numb—the avoidance symptoms of PTSD.

According to Horowitz, human beings have a natural tendency to try to keep processing information until what really happened and their internal pictures of who they are and of how the world works match. The stuffed information breaks through denial in the form of dreams, flashbacks, and obsessive thoughts. It demands attention until it has been completely processed. Again overload happens, and avoidance symptoms kick in to protect trauma survivors—until the intrusive symptoms begin all over again. Many people stay stuck in this emotional cycle for years. Eventually, though it may take many months or years of therapy, they can finish processing the trauma, so that it loses its powerful emotional charge.

Even though the *information-processing model* of PTSD formulated by Horowitz is the most commonly accepted psychological explanation for why the symptoms of PTSD occur, other psychiatrists and psychologists have added their own theories to the PTSD picture. Some of them believe that the symptoms of PTSD occur in part because they are learned through a system of rewards and punishments. When a soldier hears the sounds of a firefight, he learns to be hypervigilant and ready for action in order to protect himself. He's rewarded for this by staying alive. Later this signal becomes associated with a number of similar cues in the environment. When he hears a car backfire or a firecracker pop, he reacts automatically on the basis of what he has learned in the combat zone. A woman who has been molested as a child or raped may learn to avoid men with the same build or coloring as her attacker. The abuse or rape was a "punishment" for being in the presence of her attacker. Learning of this type is called *classical conditioning.*

Memory Repression

Usually the symptoms of PTSD begin to show themselves within three months after a trauma, but they can arise years after the initial events that triggered them. Carlos's father repressed his feelings during the heat of battle only to be overwhelmed by them 20 years later. Sometimes incest survivors completely block not only the feelings but the trauma itself from their conscious memories. Rayetta "forgot" all about being sexually abused by her mother's boyfriend when she was four. Now, years later, she has very few clues about what might have happened, so her flashbacks and nightmares are bewildering to her.   She thinks, sometimes, that she is losing her mind.

Not everyone who undergoes a trauma can remember what happened to them. Accident victims often have no conscious memory of the events they experienced. They may recall what happened right up until the time of the accident, but even though witnesses say these victims were conscious, the victims don't remember a thing until the time they arrived in the hospital.

When questioned, some trauma victims deny that they ever went through the trauma and they may even deny their symptoms. For years Carlos's dad had horrible nightmares and would awaken his wife with his screams for help. One night he even dreamed she was an enemy soldier and he tried to choke her in his sleep. When she told him how frightened she was to sleep with him, he said *she* was the one who was acting crazy—he hadn't had a dream in years.

Some researchers believe that the ability to repress memories so deeply that they are, in effect, "forgotten" may be nature's way of protecting some trauma victims. Psychologist Peretz Lavie, with the Technion-Israel Institute of Technology, recently studied people in their sixties who had survived the Holocaust in World War II when Adolf Hitler tried to exterminate the Jews by sending them to death camps. None of his research subjects had PTSD. Lavie found that most of them couldn't remember any of their dreams and denied that they even dreamed at all, despite the fact that researchers recorded periods of rapid eye movement that indicated that they were dreaming. According to Lavie, the massive unconscious repression of dream recall and the repression of memories and feelings about the trauma while they were awake had helped these Holocaust survivors to adjust to everyday life.

Some people, like Rayetta, can't clearly remember the trauma, but they are painfully aware of the symptoms, and they have a suspicion that something bad has happened to them. They just can't figure out what it was. Currently a debate is splitting the mental-health community as to whether or not "forgotten memories" like Rayetta's can be trusted to be true. This disagreement centers on childhood trauma and will be discussed in greater detail later.

Many trauma victims know that something happened to them, but they don't realize that they are victims because they haven't considered what occurred to have been a violation. Women who have been victimized often fall into this latter category. For example, a woman may be severely beaten by her husband or boyfriend, but because of the way she was raised or things her partner has said to her, she may believe that she brought the attack on herself or she may think that all men hit their partners. Because she doesn't see herself as a victim or believe that what happened really was a trauma, even though she experiences the symptoms of PTSD, she probably will not see a need to reach out for help.

Quite frequently people know they were traumatized but they don't connect their symptoms to what has happened to them. This is especially common in cases in which the symptoms don't surface until years after the emotional shock has passed. Because they were able to lead fairly normal lives in the time between the trauma and the symptoms of PTSD, they don't link the two things. Instead they may blame recent stress or another person for their current problems. Many times people who have experienced a severe stress only experience PTSD symptoms during the time of year the original trauma took place. This is called an *anniversary reaction.* Unless the people experiencing an anniversary reaction connect their symptoms to the trauma that happened to them years earlier, they, too, may blame their jumpiness, bad dreams, and short temper on something currently occurring in their lives, instead of recognizing the real source and getting help.

Secondary Wounding: The Trauma after the Trauma

Even when people are aware of the trauma that has happened to them and understand that their symptoms are caused by the emotional shock they went through, they may not receive help when they reach out for it.

When Karen expressed grief for her lost pet and began to lose interest in the life going on around her, her mother responded by telling her she should be grateful and happy. "Stop moping!" she ordered. Karen continued to act depressed and to withdraw further into her new room and her mind, which was filled with thoughts of the fire. Sometimes she tried to block thoughts of the flames and smoke from that terrible night, but those images were far more difficult to escape than the apartment fire itself. When she tried to tell her mom what was going on inside her head and to explain how scary it was to feel the way she did, her mother told her that she shouldn't cry over spilled milk. "You'll be fine if you don't dwell on the past," she advised. "Just snap out of it." When Karen heard those words of advice, she didn't feel any better. In fact, she felt worse, and she made a vow not to speak again about what was troubling her. If her own mother, who had experienced the fire, couldn't understand, she was sure nobody else would either.

Have you ever had a really big problem in your life that troubled you so much that you couldn't concentrate on your schoolwork and you didn't feel like being around people, a problem that caused you to feel very sad or angry for a few days? Did anyone tell you that you shouldn't be feeling what you couldn't help feeling? Did they tell you to snap out it, to keep a stiff upper lip or to stop talking about how you felt? How did their advice make you feel?

Many times people, like Karen, who have undergone a trauma hear that they should put the past behind them and get on with their lives. They are criticized for having the symptoms of PTSD, symptoms they can't help. They are advised to ignore their feelings, feelings that are natural after a trauma. As a result, trauma victims feel doubly hurt because it seems like no one will listen to them and no one understands what they are going through. Maybe no one even cares. The emotional pain that comes from what people say to them and how people act toward them after a trauma is called *secondary wounding.*

According to Aphrodite Matsakis, Ph.D., clinical coordinator for the Vietnam Veteran's Outreach Center in Silver Spring, Maryland, and author of *I Can't Get Over It: A Handbook for Trauma Survivors,* secondary wounding occurs when people reach out for help and encounter disbelief, denial, and discounting; when they are blamed for what happened to them; when they are made fun of, looked down on, thought to be crazy, or are punished. It happens as well when they are denied help. Secondary wounding occurs quite frequently—too frequently.

When Rayetta was very young and her mother's boyfriend was sexually abusing her, she tried telling her mother about it. Her mother angrily accused Rayetta of making the story up in order to get her new companion in trouble. Rayetta's mom washed her daughter's mouth out with soap for lying and made her stay in her room for a whole day. From this experience, Rayetta learned not to talk about what had happened. By a year later, when her mother and her boyfriend split up, Rayetta had begun to believe that maybe she was a liar, that she'd imagined everything. Maybe she'd dreamed it. By the time she was in middle school she'd denied the memories so well she had no clear idea of what was responsible for her sudden nightmares and flashbacks.

Bill thought his friends would offer him some support after he was mugged by gang members. He didn't expect sympathy, just a few words of encouragement. Instead they criticized him for not fighting back, a strategy that would have put him in more danger since he was so outnumbered. Some of the people he knew made fun of him, calling him a crybaby and a sissy for how he'd handled the crisis. He knew that if they had been in his shoes, they would have had the sense not to try and act like Rambo or Robocop either, but he kept his mouth shut. Whenever anybody brought up the gang attack, he changed the subject. Even when his nightmares began and his grades started slipping, he refused to share what was happening even with his parents or teachers. He was a man, he told himself; he could handle it on his own.

Carlos's father came back from Vietnam in 1971, a time when many people, not only the antiwar protesters, believed that the war was wrong and that it should end. Because they felt powerless to change the minds of the government and military leaders in charge of the war, some of them used the returning soldiers as targets for their anger. When Carlos's dad limped off the plane after his discharge from the army, none of his family came to the airport to meet him. They were too busy. He could understand that, but it hurt his feelings. After all, he'd been wounded and nearly killed trying to defend the beliefs they said were important to them. Now it seemed like they didn't give a hoot about what he'd been through. His feelings were hurt even more when he stopped at a bar near the airport and some of the people there called him a baby killer. What was going on? He hadn't killed any babies, only enemy soldiers who would have blown him away if he hadn't pulled the trigger first! He wouldn't even have been over there in the first place if he hadn't been drafted. On the way home, he was so angry he changed clothes and threw his uniform away with his medals still attached. From that minute on, if anybody questioned him about what had happened to him during the war, he left the room.

Most of us have a difficult time understanding why people would treat trauma victims with such cruelty. According to Matsakis, there are different reasons for disbelief, denial, and even outright rejection or hostility. Many people are ignorant about the effects that trauma has on its victims. These people really do believe that all it takes for trauma victims to feel better is to put the past behind them and get on with the business of living a normal life—two things that are impossible with PTSD. Bill's friends and most of the people at the bar who gave Carlos's dad such a horrible homecoming had never been through a traumatic event. They had no idea of the long-lasting and deep emotional scars that can follow such a severe shock. Karen's mother, although she had experienced the fire, didn't have the same reaction as her daughter. She was older and had more coping skills. For her, the trauma had an entirely different meaning. She assumed that Karen should feel the same way about what had happened as she did.

Sometimes even helping professionals like policemen, doctors, nurses, and psychological counselors—people we think should know better—treat trauma victims in ways that cause them harm. At times this treatment stems from ignorance, but often it comes from burnout. Many of these people have seen so many shootings, stabbings, rapes, auto accidents, and the victims of these traumas that they have learned to do their jobs in cold, unfeeling, mechanical ways. To be sensitive or to care too much about the people they encounter causes them to feel too much emotional pain, helplessness, and hopelessness. Some of the people in these professions suffer from PTSD themselves, because of the trauma they have experienced in the course of their work. Because of their struggle with their own untreated symptoms, it is difficult for them to give other trauma victims the emotional support and understanding they need.

Finally, most of us like to believe that we live in a just and fair world and that we can usually predict what will happen next. We assume that our lives, for the most part, are quite safe. We may read about gang violence, war, natural disasters, or rape, but many of us are convinced that these are things that happen to other people— people we don't know.

Talking with trauma victims and listening to their stories can be scary because when we do this, our assumptions are challenged. We begin to understand that bad things can, indeed, happen to people we know. They can happen to us, too. The trauma comes a little too close to home for comfort, and we realize that we aren't as safe as we thought we were.

Many people are so frightened of admitting their vulnerability to trauma either to themselves or to other people that they want their soldiers to remain silent about the fact that war is killing and death. They may tell incest survivors, like Rayetta, that they should just be quiet about what happened to them, grow up, and get over it. They refuse to listen to the stories of trauma survivors because those stories make them uncomfortable. Sometimes this discomfort comes from the fact that they may have experienced similar traumas and have either knowingly or unknowingly blocked the event from their memories. They may be in denial themselves.

When trauma victims meet with these kinds of responses and are told that they must remain silent and forget about what happened, they often feel angry. They also may begin to feel ashamed for having the symptoms of PTSD. This shame can be every bit as damaging as the trauma itself, because it causes people with PTSD to hide what they are going through from everyone, including the professionals who do care and can aid trauma victims in making their lives easier.

3

PTSD: A Multitude of Victims

Bill, Karen, Rayetta, Carlos, and his father have all seen their daily lives changed by a number of the distressing symptoms explored in the last two chapters. Even though they share a diagnosis of post-traumatic stress disorder, each of these people has lived through a very different trauma. As we've learned, many things that happen to people can be emotionally damaging enough to later spark PTSD symptoms both in them and in those who witness these traumatic events.

Traumatic events occur quite frequently in the world around us. The variety of experiences that have the potential to cause people to develop the symptoms of PTSD is wide. Diana Sullivan and Louis Everstine, authors of *The Trauma Response: Treatment for Emotional Injury* have compiled a list that includes many events and circumstances that have the potential to trigger PTSD in the people who

experience them. Although the list is a long one, undoubt-
edly people have been known to develop PTSD from things
that aren't noted here.

As you read the following list, patterned after Sullivan
and Everstine's, you may discover that you have experienced one or more of the items or something similar in
your life. You may know someone who has lived through
one of these traumas. Take a few minutes to jot down ways
in which a traumatic incident has changed your life or that
of your friend or family member. Are any of these changes
like the ones Bill, Rayetta, Karen, Carlos, or his father have
experienced?

Some Events That Can Cause PTSD

- **Disasters**   Floods, fires, earthquakes, violent storms,
  and volcanic eruptions are examples of natural disasters
  that have the potential to disrupt lives and even take
  them. Human-made disasters include such mass tragedies as collapsed buildings, airplane crashes, and wars.
  The Holocaust during World War II, when the Nazis
  killed six million Jews, is another example of a major
  disaster that was human-made. Automobile and other
  kinds of accidents, even though they may not affect a
  great number of people at one time, can cause PTSD in
  those who are involved in them and those who witness
  them as well. (According to the National Safety Council,
  in 1992, 40,300 people in the United States were killed
  in motor vehicle accidents.)
- **Physical Assaults**   This catagory of trauma includes
  violent crime, like stabbings and shootings, as well as
  terrorist acts, domestic violence, and child abuse.
- **Sexual Assaults**   Whether an adult is raped or a child
  is sexually molested, the consequences of living through
  these acts can include post-traumatic stress disorder.
- **Violent Agency**   Either willfully or accidentally causing
  death or bodily harm to another person can bring about

PTSD. A violent agent might be a driver who causes an accident in which someone is killed, an enraged ex-husband who shoots his former wife's boyfriend, or a combat soldier who must kill the enemy.

- **Bearing Witness to Tragedy** Seeing a friend, relative, or classmate killed or injured is enough to give people PTSD. Sometimes the symptoms of PTSD develop after people observe these things happen to strangers. Law-enforcement workers, ambulance drivers, and emergency room technicians tend to have higher rates of PTSD than the general population because they witness so much tragedy.

- **Property Losses** Burglary, theft, robbery, and even vandalism of property can cause crime victims to feel so threatened that the result is a severe emotional shock.

- **Physical Losses** People who lose parts of their bodies or who lose abilities they once had because of accidental injury, severe illnesses, or major surgery sometimes find these changes more than they can bear emotionally.

- **Losses by Death** The death of a spouse, child, parent, or close friend is a possible reason for developing PTSD. Even the loss of a pet, if the animal was a beloved and constant companion, may cause severe emotional shock.

- **Losses of Relationship** Love relationships or close friendships that end suddenly occasionally throw emotions in such turmoil that people develop PTSD.

- **Threats of Disaster** Disasters don't necessarily have to happen in order to cause PTSD in victims. Experiencing a death threat or having someone threaten to harm a person can cause such severe stress that the reaction is PTSD.

- **Threatened Losses.** Discovering that a friend or relative is terminally ill or having a family member kidnapped or simply disappear can be traumatic.

- **Losses of Status** Sometimes losses such as being fired, going bankrupt, or being publicly humiliated are so severe that they can cause long-term emotional damage in the form of PTSD.

As mentioned earlier, not all people who endure traumatically stressful events, even extreme ones such as wars, earthquakes, or acts of terrorism, end up with post-traumatic stress disorder. Although the exact reasons that this is true are still a mystery, psychological researchers now believe the chance of a person developing PTSD depends on many factors in addition to the meaning of the trauma to the person. Before you read further, take a few minutes to write down some explanations you might have for this part of the PTSD puzzle, based on your own life experiences and those of the people around you. Why do you think some people might be more vulnerable to extreme stress than others? What is it about some events that makes them scarier than others? Now begin reading and compare your ideas with those of PTSD researchers.

Why Some People Develop PTSD and Others Don't

Most experts in the field of trauma study today think that, given the right circumstances, severe emotional or physical shock can cause nearly anyone to develop PTSD. They are looking for clues to explain why some trauma victims may suffer from PTSD for the remainder of their lives while others seem to escape the symptoms entirely or have them disappear in time. Some of the reasons researchers are uncovering depend on the individual who has undergone the trauma.

A few researchers have begun exploring whether or not certain conditions that existed in peoples' lives before the trauma took place might make them more vulnerable to developing PTSD afterward. Some of these factors have included: mental illness in the family in which a person was raised, low self-esteem as a teenager, childhood behavior problems, and growing up in poverty. All of these factors have been shown to have some some influence on whether or not a person will develop PTSD after a trauma and on how severe their symptoms will be. Unlike earlier psychotherapists, though, today's mental-health professionals believe that while these things may raise the risk of developing PTSD, they are not *responsible* for causing it.

A person's age and how much he or she has matured emotionally at the time of the potentially traumatic event can have an impact on their chances of developing PTSD and the degree of severity of PTSD once they develop. According to psychologist Raymond Flannery, the younger and more immature the trauma victim is, the greater the likelihood that the person will suffer long-term negative consequences. The younger we are, the more easily our entire world is turned upside down because we lack experience and perspective. The older we grow, the more coping skills we develop. For this reason, very young children who are victims of sexual abuse are more likely to disassociate so much that they form multiple personalities than are older victims of the same type of trauma. Many psychologists who work for Veterans Administration hospitals believe that the reason the Vietnam War was so emotionally damaging to the soldiers who fought it was because on the average they were 19, several years younger than the men who fought in World War II.

Some biological researchers believe that certain people may be born with a physical *predisposition* to PTSD. In other words, the receptors in their brains that pick up messages transmitted by the neurochemicals cortisol, epinephrine, and norepinephrine may be more sensitive than those of other people. These people are more easily aroused than others and they remain that way for longer. Another theory is that perhaps people with a biological predisposition for PTSD may produce fewer endorphins during stress than most other people. Not only are they more sensitive to the trauma, but they are more deeply affected by the intrusive symptoms they experience later, such as nightmares and flashbacks.

Finally, people who have been traumatized before, either as children or as adults, are more vulnerable to new traumas. Once a person has experienced trauma, his or her nervous system is more sensitive. As noted earlier, lower levels of norepinephrine are needed to kindle arousal responses. For example, an incest victim who is later raped as an adult generally faces more severe problems after the rape than does a rape victim without a history of childhood trauma.

A 1991 study sponsored by the National Center for Post Traumatic Stress Disorder also provides support for the notion that one trauma leaves victims vulnerable to the next. Researchers found that Vietnam combat veterans with PTSD had higher rates of childhood physical abuse than did combat veterans who hadn't been abused as children. Although the researchers were careful to warn that the childhood beatings didn't cause combat-related PTSD later in life, they wrote, "Individuals abused in childhood may have acquired characteristic methods of coping with stressful experiences, such as emotional numbing, which may, in fact, make them more susceptible to subsequent trauma such as combat stress." Studies done on Israeli soldiers show that those who had developed PTSD symptoms after their first war were more likely than other soldiers to develop them again in later wars.

The experts who study post-traumatic stress disorder believe that many of the differences in how people react to trauma lie in the event rather than the individual. For example, the intensity of the traumatic event is one of the most important elements that determines the risk and severity of PTSD. According to the American Psychiatric Association, the more deeply an event causes us to feel fear, terror, and helplessness, the more likely it is we will develop PTSD afterward.

The events that have the most potential for causing us to develop PTSD are those that threaten our *own* lives or well-being. They tend to involve physical as well as emotional injury. In a St. Louis study of Vietnam veterans, it was learned that those soldiers who were wounded in combat were three times more likely to have PTSD than those who had fought without being injured. A 1990 study of sexual-assault victims found that rape victims who were physically injured were 23 times more likely to develop PTSD than those who had escaped such harm.

Another important factor is how long the traumatic event lasts. One emotionally shocking incident that passes in a matter of minutes is enough to cause a lifetime of emotional suffering. For example, a study reported in the *Journal of the American Medical Association* in 1988 found that 30 percent of the survivors of fatal traffic accidents and homicide attempts have PTSD. Repeated trauma over a period of time, however, leads to even higher rates of suffering. According to one study, 85 percent of the survivors of Nazi concentration camps who are still alive have post-traumatic stress disorder. A 40-year follow-up done on American soldiers who were prisoners of war in World War II, done by Kluznik, Speed, and Valkenburg, turned up the fact that 67 percent of these men still have PTSD.

How often the event has occurred can have a major influence on how a person reacts afterward as well. Military psychologists limited the time soldiers would be exposed to battle conditions during the Vietnam War to a year because the more times the soldiers faced combat, the greater were their chances of suffering emotional breakdown. Incest victims who have been repeatedly violated over a period of years tend to have much stronger reactions to the sexual assault than do children who were sexually molested only once.

Researchers Green, Wilson, and Lindy, who have studied a number of people with PTSD, have found that several trauma factors affect whether or not a person will experience PTSD. These factors also affect how quickly a person can be helped to heal from trauma. The American Psychiatric Association notes other elements that increase the risk that a person will develop PTSD after a trauma. They are combined in the following list:

- The severity of the traumatic event
- Lack of warning before the event
- Nearness to the event
- Exposure to death, especially mutilated dead bodies
- Darkness
- Experiencing the trauma alone
- Torture
- How long the trauma lasted
- How often it occurred
- The degree of loss the person experienced and how much grief they felt
- The degree to which the trauma victim was displaced from familiar surroundings
- Whether or not the person was an active or passive participant in the event
- How much control the person has over the trauma happening again

Sometimes traumas may not directly threaten us, but instead they affect our family members or close friends, or our homes or communities. Carlos has lived all of his life with a parent who has PTSD. As a result, he, too, suffers many of the same symptoms as his father. He has felt fear and helplessness for as long as he can remember.

Mental-health workers call these people *secondary victims.* Unlike primary victims who have had something traumatic actually happen to them, secondary victims are affected by having a relationship with the primary victim or by seeing the traumatic act occur, such as students who witness the suicide of a classmate. Workers who help people who have undergone trauma, such as policemen, social workers, and therapists, are often considered to be secondary trauma victims as well.

Studies show that secondary victims often have the same symptoms as those people who were directly traumatized. Unless the secondary trauma victims saw violence, death, or mutilated bodies, their symptoms may not be as severe as those of primary victims. This is because their levels of fear and helplessness during the trauma generally aren't as high as those of primary victims. Only recently have secondary trauma victims begun to receive the attention and the help they need in order to heal their emotional wounds.

While victims of any kind of extreme stress share many symptoms, different kinds of trauma tend to cause not only different rates of PTSD but slightly different ways of reacting among survivors. Because not all types of traumatic events have been studied, the remainder of this chapter will discuss those that researchers know the most about today.

Major Disasters

A tornado sweeps across the South, causing millions of dollars in property damage and killing several people, including those attending Sunday services in a church that was hit. Brushfires blaze across the Southern California foothills, burning thousands of acres and destroying many homes. Major disasters such as these happen routinely throughout the world, affecting many people. The World Health Organization, which keeps records of disasters, estimates that 1.2 million people worldwide were left homeless and 3.5 million were directly affected by hurricanes from 1900 to 1988. Earthquakes, typhoons, and cyclones affected 26 million people during that time period.

Not all disasters of major proportion are caused by the forces of nature. Some are human-made, such as the 1995 bombing of the Federal Center in Oklahoma City. Other examples of human-made disasters in addition to those listed earlier are: mass torture and nuclear reactor accidents, like the one that happened at Chernobyl in Russia. In 1992, according to the National Safety Council, 32 airplane accidents claimed the lives of 990 people in the United States. Wars are also considered to be human-made disasters. They affect not only the soldiers who fight them; for example, since the beginning of the Yugoslavian Civil War in 1991, more than 700,000 civilians, including children, have been driven out of Bosnia, their homeland.

When we hear reports about hurricanes, plane crashes, and war-torn areas, like Bosnia, or read about them in the newspapers, we learn the number of lives that were lost and the value of businesses and homes destroyed. Many people assume that the suffering of victims ends when the disaster and the news coverage ends. Rescue workers, including the Red Cross, arrive on the scene to offer help. Bodies are identified, funerals are held, and life goes on. When people have lost their homes, they are relocated, and the job of rebuilding begins. For many victims, however, the end of the disaster only marks the beginning of long-term problems.

Remember how devastated Karen felt after fire destroyed her family's apartment. Now imagine how she might have felt had the fire destroyed much of her entire community and caused her to lose friends and relatives. How would you feel if familiar landmarks in your neighborhood, like your school, the nearest convenience store, and the neighbors' homes, in addition to your own, were suddenly wiped out by forces beyond your control? Or what if many of the people you always relied upon for emotional support were no longer a part of your world? You couldn't go to them to help you sort out your emotions because they were no longer there.

People who live through major disasters face losses as great as these in addition to losing their belief that the world is an orderly and predictable place. Some disaster victims are able to get on with their lives after such a major upset, but many others develop the symptoms of post-traumatic stress disorder. Aphrodite Matsakis says of the victims of the severe 1993 Midwest floods, "There's a sense of helplessness and futility." Children who lost their homes, pets, and toys in the November 1993 California fires, which displaced 25,000 people, woke up terrified that they would lose their families for months after the flames were put out.

When psychologist Bonnie Green surveyed a number of studies on survivors of disasters that included floods, fires, tornadoes, a jet crash, and the collapse of the skywalk at the Kansas City Hyatt Regency Hotel, she found that survivors most commonly experienced sleeplessness, nightmares, and intrusive memories after the crisis had passed. Other research indicates that bad dreams are more likely to happen to people who have lost possessions or a loved one in a disaster than to those who had watched the disaster but had suffered no such losses.

The chances that someone who has survived a disaster will suffer from intrusive symptoms of PTSD become much greater if that person has seen the dead bodies of others he or she knows or if, after the crisis, that person is asked to identify those bodies for officials. Some of the other symptoms common to PTSD—shame at being alive while others have have been killed and loss of the ability to care for other people—happen to disaster victims much less frequently than they do to survivors of other types of trauma.

Other research done on disaster victims has shown that, on the whole, they are less suspicious and withdrawn than are war veterans. Some mental-health workers conclude from this that victims of natural disasters probably feel less anger than do victims of human-made disasters, who have someone to blame for their emotional pain. Even so, people who have come through earthquakes, fires, or floods may experience some anger toward the forces of nature or at what they believe is an unjust god. They also may target angry thoughts and feelings at bad warning systems and ineffective rescue workers.

Instead of developing post-traumatic stress disorder, a high number of disaster victims become depressed after the event. In a 1983 study after a Los Angeles fire, it was found that many people who had endured the tragedy felt sad, anxious, or depressed. Quite a few of these people experienced decreased appetite and enthusiasm. Psychologist Aphrodite Matsakis has found in the course of her work with disaster victims that sometimes disasters bring up memories of old traumas or times a survivor felt victimized in the past.

Some other problems that people may face after living through a disaster include: frustration and irritability, difficulty concentrating, feeling overwhelmed, as well as headaches and stomach problems caused by stress. Grief, insecurity, and an unwillingness to talk about the disaster are other possible aftereffects. Some disaster victims turn to alcohol or drugs to lower their fear that another catastrophe is right around the corner.

Mental-health workers who have studied how people cope after large-scale tragedies have found that some fearful survivors develop phobias or compulsive rituals, like never leaving the house unless they are wearing a certain item of clothing. Like Karen, some of them must check and double-check all the exits in their homes before they can sleep. Often these rituals are performed in the belief that they will prevent another disaster from happening.

Major tragedies don't always have to destroy peoples' homes and property or take lives in order to leave PTSD in their wake. For example, in 1989 a tanker ran aground off the coast of Alaska, spilling millions of gallons of oil, which washed ashore, causing serious harm to the environment. According to a study reported in the October issue of the *American Journal of Psychiatry,* members of communities affected by the *Exxon Valdez* oil spill were three times as likely to have PTSD than people living in areas that weren't affected. Of the people living in areas suffering from environmental and economic damage, women, young adults, and Native Americans seemed to suffer the highest rates of PTSD.

Although the results of research are mixed, more women than men seem to suffer from PTSD after a disaster. Psychologists aren't certain why this happens. Both men and women who develop disaster-related PTSD may suffer from it for years afterward. Fourteen years after the Buffalo Creek flood, which was caused when a West Virginia dam broke, a fourth of the people who lived through it still had PTSD.

Violent Crime

- A motorist on his way home from work is shot in the head for cutting in front of another driver on the freeway.
- A young woman is dragged from her automobile and raped in the deserted parking lot of a shopping center after she stopped there because of car trouble.
- A homeless, elderly alcoholic is stabbed to death in the alley where he is sleeping, then set on fire and left to burn.

Violent crime—including assaults, robberies, and rapes—has soared in our society. Each year more and more people become victims. In fact, a Senate Judiciary Report released in 1991 stated that crime has increased 516 percent since the 1960s. According to the National Crime Victimization Survey, conducted by the Bureau of Justice Statistics, violent crimes in the United States in 1991 rose three times faster than the overall crime rate, which includes nonviolent offenses. In that year 10.9 million violent crimes were committed. Assaults accounted for 9.1 million of these crimes, robberies for 1.3 million, and sexual assaults for

484,000. The rate of children murdered quadrupled from 1983 to 1993, according to the Federal Bureau of Investigation Uniform Crime Report.

In fact, the risks children in the United States face are so high that the Children's Defense Fund has called for a "cease fire" in the violence. According to their 1994 yearbook, between 1979 and 1991, almost 50,000 children died from being shot. This total equals American casualties during the Vietnam War. In 1991 alone, there were twice as many children under 10 killed by guns than American soldiers killed in the Persian Gulf War. The Children's Defense Fund reports that a child living in the United States is 15 times as likely to be killed by firearms as a child in Northern Ireland. A child dies from gunshot wounds every two hours in the United States. A police officer meets the same fate every five days and nine hours.

Not only are violent-crime rates soaring, but the pattern of crime in the United States is changing as well. For as long as law-enforcement officials have kept statistics, they have found that the majority of violent crimes were committed by people who knew their victims, usually family members or friends. Whether motivated by anger or jealousy, or greed, these crimes seemed to have been committed for a reason. Not so today. According to the FBI Uniform Crime Report, in 1993 random acts of violence committed by strangers outnumbered violent acts between people who knew one another. "Every American now has a realistic chance of being murdered because of the random nature the crime has assumed," states the report. The report goes on to say that "this trend has generated profound fear of murder victimization."

It is no wonder that the Justice Department reported in 1988 that only a third of the people in the United States feel safe in their neighborhoods. Sometimes it seems as if there is nowhere to hide. The FBI found that although large cities still have the highest homicide rates, during the first part of 1993, small towns experienced the largest increases in the number of reported killings. An estimated five out of six Americans will become victims of violent crimes at some point in their lifetimes.

When people compare the crime wave to living in a battle zone, they may be right. Researchers have found that the highest rates of PTSD, next to combat veterans, are the result of physical attack. According to psychologists Dean Kilpatrick and Heidi Resnick, the number of people who experience PTSD after being the targets of violent crime is high. The chance of developing PTSD range from 1 in 3 to 6 in 10 after physical assault. PTSD rates for people who were robbed or burglarized range between 17 percent and 28 percent. Of all violent crimes, rape leaves the highest rates of post-traumatic stress disorder in its wake. If a person's life is threatened or if he or she is physically injured by the crime, then the chance of developing PTSD doubles. It quadruples when both factors are present.

Losing a family member to violent crime can also cause emotional problems to surface later. From 25 percent to 71 percent of people who have had a relative murdered develop PTSD. Rates of PTSD are highest when the victim was a child or when more than one person was murdered. Even seeing a violent crime committed can leave people to struggle with post-traumatic stress disorder. Witnesses of assault have relatively low rates of PTSD, but when the aggravated assault is on a family member, the rate jumps to 62.5 percent.

Most violent-crime victims experience what psychologists call *acute trauma reaction* right after the event, showing some PTSD symptoms and a range of emotions from depression to rage. This reaction usually has several stages. The first is shock. Once numbness wears off, however, the impact stage begins. At this point a crime victim may feel powerless and overwhelmed by feelings such as fear, grief, rage, shame, and a desire for revenge. During the attribution stage, victims and the people around them try to make meaning from the crime by trying to guess why it happened and by placing blame either on the person who committed the crime or on the victim. For example, a woman who was raped by a man who broke into her house might mistakenly blame herself for what happened, telling herself that she should have installed stronger locks or that she shouldn't have been wearing her bathrobe. In the last stage, resolution, the crime victim regains balance.

Unless a crime victim goes through the resolution stage, his or her chances of developing PTSD are high. The most common long-term symptoms violent-crime victims experience are: hypervigilance, intrusive memories, sleep disturbances, and startle responses. Often their victimization causes them to lose trust in people, so they withdraw from others. This is especially true if they know the person who tried to harm them.

In addition to PTSD, many crime victims develop *phobias,* intense and unreasonable fears. A woman who has been raped might not want to be touched by any man, not even her husband, even though he has never done anything to hurt her. A mugging victim like Bill might develop *agoraphobia,* a fear of going outside his house for any reason.

Domestic Violence

Think about a time a complete stranger said something insulting to you. Maybe that person accused you of being rude or told you that you were making too much noise and that you should shut up. Perhaps somebody who didn't know you made a comment implying that you didn't know what you were doing or weren't very smart. Now think about a time somebody you cared a great deal about became angry with you and said something insulting. Which event hurt your feelings the most and made you feel worse about yourself?

Violent crime randomly committed by strangers leaves one kind of emotional scarring—fear that the world is a totally unpredictable place in which something horrible could happen at any instant. Being deliberately attacked by a person to whom you are emotionally close—someone you love and who tells you that they love you—leaves another kind of damage: low self-esteem and the tendency to blame yourself for the assault. When people who say they love us turn around and hurt us with words or with physical violence, the emotional damage we suffer is often deeper and longer lasting than that experienced when someone we never met before tries to hurt us in those same ways.

In 1991 an estimated 1,370,700 adult domestic violence cases were reported in the United States. In each instance, one partner in a married, living-together, or dating relationship assaulted the other person in that relationship. Although some men are battered, the majority of adult domestic violence victims are women. The severest physical injuries most frequently occur in instances when men are the batterers and women are the victims because men usually have the advantage in size and strength.

Sometimes violent arguments that become abusive end in death. Indications that a love relationship with another person is life-endangering are:

- The use of weapons like guns or knives
- Being choked
- Being thrown into objects
- Being forcefully shaken
- Having one's head banged against a hard surface
- Hearing threats against one's life

Domestic violence counselors report that women's lives tend to be in the most danger once they decide to end the relationship and begin making attempts to leave. This is why shelters and safe houses do not make their addresses public. This is also one of the reasons that victims stay in abusive relationships—they are afraid they will be killed if they try to go and are caught by their abusers. Victims of battering also sometimes stay with their abusers out of fear they will lose their children if they leave or because they are dependent on the batterer for food and shelter.

Although not all domestic violence victims suffer from PTSD even after experiencing the extreme violence detailed above, many of them do. Battering incidents that are reported to the police usually involve physical assaults such as those listed above or punching, kicking, and slapping. However, battering can take a number of other forms of manipulation and control which cause PTSD among victims as well. Economic control, social isolation, emotional abuse, threats of physical harm, and sexual assaults between people who are married can also cause post-traumatic stress disorder. In addition to physical assault, the American Psychiatric Association lists sexual abuse and psychological torture high on its list of stressors.

How would you feel if someone who claimed to love you made you stay home all day and accused you of seeing someone else romantically when you went to the grocery store for 15 minutes? What if they didn't trust you to make a phone call or even talk with your family? What if they wouldn't give you any money, even for a pack of chewing gum or a pair of new shoes when your old ones wore out? What if they kept you awake nights with loud and angry speeches about how ugly you were? If you are like most people, after months or years of this treatment, you would feel anxious, and you would begin to doubt your worth as a person. Maybe you'd even think that no one else could ever love you.

One of the reasons that battering, both emotional and physical, causes PTSD is that it tends to be repeated over and over again in a relationship, happening in a certain pattern which counselors call the *domestic violence cycle.* Tension begins building in the relationship and is followed by either physical or emotional battering. Typically, after the abuse is over, the batterer tries to "make it up" to the victim for a time and may give that person compliments and even presents. Usually the battering incident is never mentioned. This is called the *honeymoon phase.* The honeymoon phase ends when tension begins building again, once more leading to a battering incident.

During the past two decades, domestic violence victims who sought treatment were said to suffer from *battered woman syndrome,* a group of psychological symptoms first written about by Dr. Lenore Walker, an expert on spouse abuse. Over the years, Walker and other professionals in the field began to notice that many of the signs of battered woman syndrome are the same as the symptoms of PTSD listed by the American Psychiatric Association. These include recurring thoughts of previous abuse and the use of numbing to avoid dealing with the situation. "Most battered women learn a mild form of self-hypnosis or dissociation to keep from experiencing the intensity of pain during the physically abusive incidents," reports Walker.

Recently, some domestic violence counselors and re-searchers, including Walker, have been attempting to con-vince other mental-health professionals to diagnose victims of battering as having PTSD. They believe that when this is done, the emphasis will be squarely placed on the trauma of being battered. They feel that, perhaps then, society will stop the secondary wounding of blaming battering victims by telling those who reach out for help that they must have done something to provoke it or accusing them of staying because they like being beaten.

Combat

The "bush vets" live hidden in the jungle on the island of Hawaii. PTSD counselors estimate there are several hun-dred of them, living in tents or makeshift "hooches," shelters like they made for themselves during the Vietnam War.

Some simply want to be left alone. Their PTSD symptoms are so severe that they cannot live among other people. For many the war has never ended; they still carry rifles and set booby traps around their camps. Other bush vets have settled in remote and isolated areas of Washington State, Maine, and Texas. They continue to be emotional hostages of a war that ended 20 years ago.

Wars cause mental suffering to *all* of the people this form of violence touches. Except for prisoners of war and concentration camp survivors, combat veterans seem to be the most affected by PTSD. As a general rule, the more combat a veteran was exposed to and the more intense that combat was, the more likely the former soldier is to suffer from PTSD. One Veterans Administration psychiatrist has called PTSD an occupational hazard of war.

Several factors make wars especially traumatic to the soldiers who fight them:

- Soldiers are separated from their homes and families. Those who fight in foreign countries are faced with a different culture and language.
- For the most part, soldiers are young men who are still in the process of learning coping skills.
- During a war, especially in a battle zone, the threat of being killed or wounded is always present.
- Battlefield conditions are physically stressing. Often soldiers march for days in extreme temperatures. Food and water may be scarce, and sleep scarcer. All this marching takes place while carrying a 40-pound pack.
- Military training encourages soldiers to hate the enemy and teaches those who will fight wars to take out their anger at the enemy by trying to kill them. It discourages compassion and caring.
- War involves seeing dying and wounded people up close. Many times soldiers saw the mutilated bodies of their friends, but to survive had to stuff their anger and grief inside.

- A situation of killing another person or being killed is perhaps the most difficult one in which a moral human being can find him- or herself. Most us have been taught from childhood that killing is wrong, yet we have an urge for self-preservation.

An estimated 15 percent of the soldiers who were in Vietnam have PTSD today. Most of them, although they may have flashbacks and difficulty dealing with their anger, do not commit violent acts against other people. Even though it is a popular stereotype, a wild-eyed vet opening fire on a crowd of people during a flashback is the very rare exception rather than the rule. This stereotype is one example of the secondary wounding that adds to the problems of combat veterans.

Although PTSD affects combat veterans more than it does former military people who did not actually fight on a battlefield, former soldiers who helped to transport the dead and wounded, medical workers, soldiers who processed the bodies, and military personnel who served in or near where the fighting went on can and do suffer from post-traumatic stress disorder.

According to the V.A., an estimated 210,000 World War II veterans, now in their 70s and 80s, still live with PTSD symptoms. Many of them have never connected the problems they have struggled with for most of their lives to their military service. Some of them refuse to share their war experiences with others even today, 40 to 50 years after their military service. Since PTSD wasn't officially recognized as a problem until decades after World War II ended, it isn't surprising that most of these veterans have never received treatment.

The most studied group of former soldiers are the veterans who served in Southeast Asia during the Vietnam War, which ended in 1975. According to a congressional study conducted by the Research Triangle Institute, nearly half a million Vietnam Veterans can be diagnosed as having post-traumatic stress disorder. An additional 350,000 live with at least some of the symptoms of PTSD.

Vietnam veterans faced additional stressors beyond the ones their fathers and uncles endured during World War II and the Korean War. As we mentioned before, soldiers sent to Vietnam were younger than those in previous wars. During Vietnam, troop rotations, which made a one-year tour of duty possible, meant that people were constantly coming and going. It was difficult to know whom to trust, and an "every man for himself" mentality developed. Most Vietnam veterans, unlike World War II vets, lost contact with their buddies after the war.

The purpose of the war was unclear both to the soldiers and to the American people. Many combat soldiers fought because they were drafted or because friends who had joined the service had been killed. The United States citizens had mixed feelings about the war, which dragged on and on without a clear victory. Too often they took their frustrations out on the returning troops when they were withdrawn, sometimes even calling soldiers "baby killers" and spitting on them.

For this reason many Vietnam veterans have spent their lives hiding the fact that they were in the war and refusing to talk about what happened to them. Counselors who work with Vietnam combat veterans have found that many of them are isolated. While a few have become bush vets, many others simply keep to themselves or move from place to place, like Carlos's dad. Hypervigilance, guilt at surviving when other soldiers were killed, nightmares, and flashbacks are also hallmarks of war-related PTSD.

Rage is another problem combat veterans face. Anger, coupled with the knowledge that they are capable of killing, keeps many vets in isolation and gets others into trouble. Some of the rage comes from the battlefield. Vietnam was a *guerrilla war,* a war fought against small, independent groups of fighters who knew the jungles and could move quickly, hiding themselves well. The North Vietnamese used land mines and booby traps. A soldier might watch one or several of his companions be blown to bits after tripping a concealed wire attached to a grenade hidden in tall grass, but the enemy would be nowhere in sight. There was no target upon which to release the anger these soldiers felt. Sometimes, in addition to living through these battle-field conditions, a veteran's anger comes from receiving a less-than-welcoming homecoming.

A 1988 study done by the American Legion and Columbia University uncovered some interesting facts about Vietnam veterans and PTSD. When they studied 2,858 members of the American Legion who had served in Southeast Asia during the Vietnam War, they found that those who had experienced high levels of combat:

- Earned $2,740 less per year than other veterans of the same age and education who didn't see combat;
- were four times as likely to be divorced as noncombat veterans;
- had more problems with depression, anxiety, irritation, and feelings of helplessness than noncombat vets;
- smoked, drank, and used drugs more often than other veterans; and
- had more stress-related health problems, such as high blood pressure and ulcers, than their peers who weren't in battle.

Veterans of all wars who seek help for themselves and their families often must do battle once again to get it. This time, their fight is against red tape. Those who are unable to work because of war injuries or emotional problems related to PTSD and who file claims so that they can receive disability payments face a long wait. The Veterans Admini-stration estimates that by the end of 1995 there will be a backlog of more than 800,000 disability claims yet to be acted upon.

Although the Veterans Administration now recognizes PTSD and works to treat it, waiting lists for PTSD programs at V.A. hospitals are long. It isn't uncommon for a veteran to wait for over a year to get needed emotional help. The American Legion claims that some of these programs don't last as long as they need to in order to effectively help vets because the government is trying to save money. As veterans who served in Grenada, Desert Storm, and Somalia begin to develop symptoms of PTSD and visit V.A. hospitals in search of assistance, the problems of dealing with the emotional casualties of war that these facilities now have are only expected to increase.

4

Young Victims: Children and PTSD

The hot afternoon sun beat down on the school bus on July 15, 1976, as the bus made its way along backcountry roads dropping off young passengers from the Dairyland School District's summer school program. The kids probably didn't mind the heat because they were still wet from swimming, the last activity of the day in a program that was more like summer camp than real school.

Several miles outside of Chowchilla, California, the bus driver slowed as he approached a white van that was parked so that it half-blocked the narrow road. Maybe if he slowed enough, he could edge the school bus past the obstacle. Suddenly a masked gunman jumped from the van, ordering the driver to stop and open the door.

The frightening man ordered the 26 young passengers to the back of the bus and told them to "shut up!" Another strange man got behind the wheel and began to drive, while a third followed in the van that had served as a roadblock. The new "bus driver" kept driving until he stopped at a remote area where the children were ordered off the bus and into two vans, a white one and a green one. The school bus was abandoned.

It was dark and crowded in the vans. A partition blocked the children from seeing or communicating with the driver so they couldn't tell him how hungry they were or how much they needed to go to the bathroom. Their trip in the mobile prison lasted 11 hours.

Finally, at three in the morning, the children were ordered out of the vans and marched one by one to something that looked like a tent, where they were questioned about their names. The man doing the questioning took something from every child—a toy, a lunchpail, an item of clothing. Then one by one, the kids were ordered to climb down into a hole.

The "hole" turned out to be a buried semitrailer that was lit by flashlights. Only a little air circulated from the movement of a tiny fan. Extremely hungry, the children began to eat the stale Cheerios, damp potato chips, and the peanut butter their kidnappers had left out for them. After the children used the makeshift bathrooms provided for them, the hole began to smell bad. Suddenly, how the place smelled didn't seem so important to them as they heard dirt and gravel being shoveled on top of the trailer. They were being buried alive.

As if that weren't bad enough, several hours later a boy leaned against a piece of board the kidnappers had used to prop up the roof of the trailer so that it wouldn't collapse under the weight of all the dirt that had been shoveled on top. The roof began to cave in. Now the kids thought they would die for sure. Two boys, one 10 and one 14, managed to slide back a metal plate which blocked the entrance to the trailer, and they began to tunnel, digging for their lives. Hours later the children escaped. They had been buried in an old rock quarry about a hundred miles from Chow-chilla.

Most of us like to think of childhood as a carefree, happy time. For many youngsters it is. For some, like the young bus passengers in Chowchilla, life is changed forever by a traumatic event. Young children are not immune from experiencing or witnessing tragedy and violence. They experience car wrecks, natural disasters, and the effects of war just as adults do. Our world is becoming a violent one. Too often children are victims. Sometimes the violence happens as a result of war. Other times children become victims at the hands of their parents or fellow classmates.

- According to the United Nations Children's Relief Fund, 1.5 million children have been killed throughout the world in the past 10 years as a result of war; more than 4 million have been physically disabled, and 5 million now live in refugee camps; 12 million have lost their homes.
- The estimated number of child-abuse victims rose 40 percent between 1985 and 1991, according to the National Committee for the Prevention of Child Abuse.
- In 1991, 358,846 children were victims of physical abuse.
- A child is battered every one and a half minutes in the United States.
- Also in 1991, 127,853 children were sexually abused in the United States, one every four minutes.
- A study done by sociologist Diana Russell in 1983 discovered that 28 percent of adult women had experienced incest or sexual abuse from a stranger before they were 14. Other researchers estimate that from 5 to 20 percent of all boys are molested.
- Nine percent of all eighth-graders carry a gun, knife, or club to school, according to a 1992 University of Michigan study.

- Children under 18 are over twice as likely to be killed by guns than they were in 1986, show statistics from the U.S. Uniform Crime reports.
- One in six youngsters between ages 10 and 17 has seen or knows someone who has been shot, according to a recent Children's Defense Fund poll.

Just because children cannot put their experiences or feelings into words, does not mean they are unmarked by trauma. When two classmates were shot outside of Long-fellow Elementary School in Bridgeport, Connecticut, in January 1993, the students were traumatized. "Kids didn't want to go to class, they couldn't eat or sleep, they burst out crying," reported principal Jettie Tisdale in a *Time* magazine interview.

Childhood Trauma—A Long Ignored Problem

Even though the number of children exposed to violence is increasing in our society, child abuse and crime have always existed to some degree. Wars and natural disasters like floods and tornadoes have never been selective in claiming their victims. However, only within the past 20 years have researchers and therapists begun to understand that children can be emotionally wounded by severe trauma and that they may need just as much help, or more, to overcome it as adults do.

Before the Chowchilla kidnapping took place in 1976, both parents and mental-health professionals believed that children were too young to be affected by trauma. According to the thought of the time, if a child was hurt, sexually molested,or witnessed tragedy, he or she would forget all about it, so long as the parents didn't talk about the event. Once the trauma was erased from memory, the child would have no lasting emotional scars.

When children did show signs of emotional upset months or years after the traumatic event had passed, psychiatrists and psychologists said it was only because their *parents* were anxious and upset. Somehow the children had "caught" this anxiety from the important adults in their lives. In fact, a World War II study done on children who had been evacuated from London when the Nazis bombed that city showed that those with calm parents adjusted better emotionally than those with nervous parents. This seemed to confirm the notion that how children reacted to severe stress depended only on how their parents reacted, not on how the trauma had affected the children personally.

In 1945 David Levy, a New York City psychiatrist, observed children who had undergone surgery and noted that some of them experienced nightmares and felt fearful. He commented that their reactions were similar to those shown by World War II soldiers who had been evacuated from the battlefield for battle fatigue. For the most part his work was ignored.

The first real study of stress and children came years later after a tornado in Vicksburg, Mississippi, flattened an elementary school. Researchers from the National Institute of Mental Health did the study in 1956, three years after the tornado. Even though they suspected that the children might be affected by witnessing this natural disaster, they didn't question the kids. Instead, they talked to their parents, asking them how the children had reacted.

The next major study of trauma and children was conducted after a 1966 disaster in Aberfan, a small town in Wales where a slag heap, a huge pile of rock, had slid down the side of a mountain, destroying the elementary school. One hundred and sixteen children died in the tragedy. National Health Service psychiatrist Gaynor Lacey treated 56 child survivors and wrote down the reactions he saw in those children. Their play had become grim and serious, he noted, and there were changes in their personality. Because he studied the children themselves and didn't rely on what their parents said, for the first time mental-health professionals began to take the effects of trauma on children seriously.

In 1972 a dam on Buffalo Creek in West Virginia broke, flooding the town of Buffalo Creek and killing 125 people. C. Janet Newman, a Cincinnati professor, interviewed children who had survived the flood. Some of them had lost a friend or relative in the disaster. Newman discovered that these kids daydreamed about death and disfigurement. They were gloomy about life, and they felt vulnerable—as though something else bad might happen to them at any moment. She concluded that the 224 child survivors of Buffalo Creek were "significantly or severely emotionally impaired."

Then, in 1976, the 26 children from Chowchilla, California, were kidnapped on their way home from school. After the kids returned home, town officials announced they were fine and a local child psychiatrist assured parents that only 1 of the 26 tragedy survivors might have emotional problems as a result of the kidnappings. Five months later, despite the fact that the kidnappers were caught and put in jail, the children still seemed jumpy. Reporters from a Fresno paper had even written an article about how parents were complaining that their kids were suffering from horrible nightmares and intense fears.

The newspaper article resulted in psychiatrist Lenore Terr being asked to spend time with the children and their parents. Maybe she could help them. For eight years she had wanted to do a study on child trauma victims, one that would take children and their reactions seriously. Perhaps this would be her chance. It was.

Terr interviewed the Chowchilla children as well as children from neighboring towns who hadn't been involved in the kidnapping in order to compare the two groups. Then she returned to Chowchilla four years later in order to talk with the children and their families once again. From the information she gathered, Terr learned much about childhood trauma. In her own words, "It was becoming clear that horrible life experiences could scar the minds of children. Many youngsters were living for years with unrecognized traumatic effects. One could not pick up a newspaper without finding a new day-care-center exposé, a child-witnessed shoot-out, or a kidnapping. I began to wonder if a generalized epidemic of psychic trauma was rampant in the world of kids."

The first results from Terr's landmark study of children and trauma were published in 1979. The research by other psychiatrists and psychologists that followed confirmed her suspicions that PTSD was widespread. A 1985 study of 50 children who were disaster victims, 50 who were victims of physical abuse, and 50 victims of child molestation showed that 77 percent of these children had PTSD. When the same number of adults who were trauma victims were studied, only 57 percent of them suffered the symptoms of PTSD.

Another study of 300 children who had been sexually molested showed that when the children were older than six, every one of them met the American Psychiatric Association's standards for PTSD. Yet another study, conducted in 1986, revealed that of 16 kids who had seen a parent murdered or attempt to murder family members, every one had PTSD after the event. According to psychologist K. C. Peterson, writing in *Post-Traumatic Stress Disorder: A Clinician's Guide,* "While the vast majority of writing on PTSD has been about soldiers, it may be that children are the foremost victims of PTSD. Depending on the type of trauma, incident rates range from 40–100 percent."

One result of the research done on children and PTSD has been that today psychologists understand that children and young people often need emotional support after an emotional shock. They also know that kids don't always have to be directly involved in a traumatic incident to suffer emotional damage from what has gone on. Even if a student doesn't actually witness a classmate's death, that child can later develop PTSD symptoms, depending on how well he or she knew the young victim. Many schools now have *trauma teams,* trained teachers and mental-health professionals who begin helping students from the minute they learn that a classmate has committed suicide or died in an auto accident.

One trailblazing program, sponsored by the Centre for International Peace Studies at McMaster University in Ontario, Canada, sends teams of psychiatrists to conflict-torn areas in the world so that they can help children cope with the emotional, as well as the physical, damage war has caused them. These groups have been called mental-health SWAT teams. Their goal is to help mental-health professionals recognize the symptoms of PTSD in children and set up programs to treat them.

The Continuing Silence

Even though professionals are now well-aware of the emotional damage trauma too often causes young people, some parents and educators, still believe that if they ignore a child or young adult's nightmares and dark daydreams, then those symptoms will go away. Some of them mistakenly think that by refusing to talk with their child about the trauma and acting as though nothing out of the ordinary has happened, they are being calm and that their silence is actually helping. Even though they allowed Dr. Terr to talk with their children, none of the Chowchilla parents took their children for therapy to get help for their PTSD symptoms. They were certain their kids would "grow out of it."

That's what Karen's mom believed after the apartment fire. Whenever Karen tried to talk about how much she missed her cat and her old belongings, her mom would either tell her she shouldn't be feeling that way or change the subject completely. As Karen became more and more withdrawn, her mother blamed her changes on hormones. "All teenage girls go through moody stages," she told herself. The longer Karen's withdrawal lasted, the more irritated her mom became with her. Her mom's anger caused Karen to pull away from people even more. Now most of the time she and her mother aren't speaking.

Bill's mother reacted in the opposite way. The minute he walked through the door after the mugging, she became hysterical. "My baby! My baby," she started screaming. Later, when she talked with the police, even they couldn't calm her down. For weeks afterward, all she could talk about was how the gang members had beaten her son, and to Bill's embarrassment, she told the tale to perfect strangers. When Bill saw how his mother was taking it, he became even more determined to live his life as if nothing happened. His six-year-old brother, who had been staying at a friend's house the night Bill was waylaid, began wetting the bed and waking up screaming. He was so afraid of "bad people" getting him that he wouldn't even play in the backyard alone anymore.

Next to the traumatic event itself, a parent's reaction to that event has the most powerful influence on how a child or young person deals with the emotional shock. According to the American Academy of Child & Adolescent Psychiatry, "The way children see and understand their parents' response is very important. Children are aware of their parents' worries most of the time but they are particularly sensitive during a crisis. Parents should admit their concerns to their children, and also stress their abilities to cope with the situation." When parents panic after a traumatic event, they increase a child's distress. When they remain silent and pretend the trauma never happened, they often increase a child's sense of shame at having been victimized.

Many adults don't like to think about how stressful everyday life can be for young people today. Teenagers have many fears that most adults are completely unaware of. Take a little time to list the things *you* might have been afraid of when you were younger. Next list the things you fear or worry about today. Finally, write down things you get anxious about when you think about the future. Now compare them to the results of a 1994 Yankelovich Youth Monitor survey of youths ages 9 through 17.

- 42 percent worry that they might contract the AIDS virus
- 32 percent fear they may some time be hurt in a car wreck
- 28 percent are afraid that they may be attacked or beaten up
- 24 percent worry that they will have to fight in a war someday

Because many grownups pay little attention to childhood stress and the fears that stress causes, it is no wonder that sometimes, even after an out-of-the-ordinary traumatic event, parents ignore the signs that indicate that a child or teenager is suffering from PTSD. They deny that a disaster has had any negative impact on their children because these adults have a difficult time coping with the notion that the world could inflict such pain on children—especially their own. In an 1982 study of preschool children after a blizzard and a flood, parents were given a checklist. They indicated on individual questions that their children's behavior had changed in negative ways after these natural disasters, but when they were asked more general questions about how their children had reacted to the storm, not one of them said that the storm had any negative effects on their children.

Sometimes parents are unaware that their children are suffering from PTSD because very young children aren't able to put their feelings into words since they haven't yet learned to talk. Even a child who has learned to talk may completely stop speaking after a traumatic event.

Older children and teenagers, too, can have a very difficult time expressing themselves or they may deliberately hide their feelings about what has gone on in their lives, refusing to discuss what happened to them. Adults often believe this silence means that the child has forgotten the traumatic incident, so parents think they will hurt their children if they bring the subject up.

Another reason that parents and teachers may not be aware that children have PTSD is that children's symptoms of prolonged reaction to severe trauma are sometimes different from those adults experience. For example, according to Lenore Terr, when children are in the middle of terrifying traumatic situations, they don't look or act very differently than they normally do, despite the fact their emotions are in turmoil. The Chowchilla children told Terr, though, that during the kidnapping, they felt afraid of their helplessness and of being separated from their loved ones. They also said they feared that something even more frightening was going to happen and that they would die.

Because most children with PTSD don't suffer intrusive flashbacks, they can concentrate more easily than adults whose flashbacks interrupt their thoughts. Terr and other researchers have found that, when the traumatic event is a one-time occurrence, children's schoolwork usually doesn't suffer, except for perhaps at most a few months after the trauma. This leads parents and teachers to sometimes conclude that everything is fine with a child when it really isn't.

Symptoms of Childhood PTSD

The symptoms that indicate that a child has PTSD differ depending on his or her age and stage of development when the trauma happened. A 1994 study, conducted by psychiatrist Christopher J. Lonigan, who interviewed 5,687 schoolchildren after Hurricane Hugo, found that younger children are more apt to develop PTSD after a disaster than older kids.

Many of the PTSD symptoms that children suffer, in addition to the absence of flashbacks, are very different from those of adults. Carlos's little sister, who can't yet use very many words, began sucking her thumb after their father pushed her down the basement stairs. When her mother leaves her at day care, she screams for hours at a time. Bill's little brother has nightmares and is terrified of being alone. Their troubles demand immediate attention from adults. According to Terr's research, children over the age of three or four rarely suffer amnesia, completely forgetting the one-time trauma they have endured. "Children generally accept horrors more easily than adults," she concluded after her study of the young kidnapping victims from Chowchilla. "Adults use more immediate denial." Children, especially older children, do consciously put the trauma out of their minds.

Instead of experiencing denial, children often *deliberately* try to rid their minds of all thoughts of the traumatic incident and of the feelings that arise when they have these thoughts. By making a decision to avoid thinking or talking about what they've gone through, they try to heal their wounds and to appear as if everything is fine. This conscious pushing aside of thoughts and feelings is different from denial, disassociation, or emotional numbing because it is a conscious decision.

Some of the general changes in behavior that indicate a child may be suffering from PTSD are listed below. According to the American Academy of Child and Adolescent Psychiatry, these symptoms can appear soon after the traumatic event, but they may surface months or even years later.

- **Clinging to adults.** Some children with PTSD will follow a parent around the house, never letting the parent out of their sight. Often this happens because the child fears that any separation, even a brief one, will turn out to be permanent. The child may even refuse to return to school.

- **Persistent phobias or fears.** Sometimes a child with PTSD is afraid of events or things that remind him or her of the trauma. A child who has been in a car wreck may be terrified of riding in cars or even crossing the street. A child who watched a young friend struck by lightning might hurry indoors at the first sign of rain. According to Terr's work, children who have endured trauma also often fear the mundane—everyday things which have no relationship to the trauma. Fear of being alone in the dark, strangers, and unexpected noises are examples of mundane fears.

- **Sleep problems.** Nightmares, screaming during sleep, bed-wetting, and sleepwalking that continue more than several days after the traumatic event are also signs of PTSD. Often the nightmares are repeated several times in a night or for several nights. Sometimes these bad dreams are exact replays of the trauma. Other nightmares are about the trauma but change what has actually happened around, as if the child's mind is trying to heal itself in sleep. Some trauma dreams change the event so much that when the child talks about them, they don't seem to have anything to do directly with what has happened to the child. An example of this might be dreaming of being chased by monsters. After a severe emotional shock, some children have terrifying dreams that they can't remember when they awaken. Researchers believe that very young children who have undergone trauma don't have nightmares.

- **Behavior problems.** After a traumatic event, some children become irritable, while others suddenly begin misbehaving in school or at home, acting out feelings of anger by doing and saying things that are unusual for them. The anger children feel after being traumatized can also lead them to play more aggressively, hitting other children or bossing them around. Researchers believe that most traumatized children feel some anger after the event, if only because of the chemical changes high levels of stress put their brains through. When they have no outlet for this feeling, the anger persists. If the child was angry before the trauma, his or her anger may turn to rage. Human-made traumas, such as violent crimes or kidnappings, like the one the Chowchilla children endured, seem to provoke more angry reactions in child victims than do natural disasters like floods or hurricanes.

- **Physical problems.** In the weeks and months after a child has been traumatized, he or she may complain of stomachaches, headaches, or dizziness. When the child is examined by a doctor, physical causes for these ailments cannot be found. Traumatized children aren't making these symptoms up. Instead, their physical problems are usually caused by extreme stress. For example, researchers have discovered that children who produce high levels of endorphins in response to trauma, such as incest, often complain of stomachaches. They believe these stomachaches may be caused by the neurochemical.

- **Withdrawal and preoccupation with the trauma.** Children who have endured trauma may pull back from family and friends, much like Bill and Karen did. They often appear listless as though they have little or no energy. Their activity level decreases and they suffer from lack of concentration. Many of the things they enjoyed doing in the past give them no pleasure.

  Like Karen, their minds may wander, their thoughts turning to the traumatic event many times throughout the day. Although the vast majority of traumatized children don't have intrusive flashbacks like adults do, they do daydream about the horrible thing that has happened to them. These daydreams, according to

Terr, come when a child's mind is at rest and is unoccupied with other things, such as schoolwork. Even though a child's daydreams may be very vivid and frightening, they don't interrupt normal daily life. Some of the Chowchilla children said that they felt "haunted" by these daydreams after the kidnapping.

- **Repeated reenactment.** Children often make-believe they are going through the traumatic event. A child who has been in an automobile accident may play car wreck over and over again. A child who has been physically abused might beat her dolls and scold them, using the same words a parent has said to her. Even though children say they are having fun when they play this way, adults who watch them often use words like grim and serious to describe the children's behavior at play.

  When Carlos was younger he used to play "army man." In fact, that was all he ever wanted to play. Many of his friends did the same thing, but they didn't play the game in quite the same way as Carlos. He would be the sergeant and scream abuse at his pretend troops for as long as they would take it before deserting him to play with other kids. "You're no good," he would holler, his face turning red with rage. "You can't do anything right and you're going to get us all killed." The words he used were almost the same as the things his dad yelled at him when he got angry at Carlos when the boy didn't guess what his dad expected of him without being told. Even when Carlos's friends suggested other games that might be more fun to play than army man, Carlos refused to play them. It seemed as if he couldn't stop.

- **Regression.** Young children sometimes seem to move back through stages in their development after experiencing a traumatic event. A child who was toilet-trained may lose control and need to wear diapers again. Behaviors like thumb-sucking, rocking back and forth, or refusing to speak may appear. Older children may begin talking baby talk or refuse to go to sleep without a teddy bear or an old blanket they slept with when they were younger.

- **Foreshortened future.** While most children seldom think about death and rarely consider that someday they may die, children who have undergone severe traumas think about these things quite a bit. Many of them believe they will die young. Often they don't talk about what they want to do when they grow up, because they have a sense of dread that they will not survive until adulthood.

Repeated Victimization

The seriousness of the PTSD symptoms a child develops after a traumatic event depends on the same things adult PTSD depends upon—whether the child witnessed the event or was caught right in the middle of it, how much trauma the child was exposed to, the severity of the event, and the degree of violence involved. Perhaps the most important factor that influences how a child will react to trauma is whether the trauma happened only once or if it occurred over and over again, as incest and physical child abuse and battering usually do.

For example, many children feel angry after they have been traumatized, but when the trauma happens over and over and was done to them by another person whom they know and have trusted, children's rage can be especially strong. A child who has been repeatedly abused may come up with one of three ways to deal with his or her anger. Some children identify with the aggressor. If they were hurt, they may hurt other children when they play. If they were sexually abused, they may molest younger children.

Other children try to work through their anger after repeated trauma by becoming passive and acting out old victimizations over and over again, either through play or in real life. These kids might allow a playground bully to terrorize them or put themselves in situations where they are in danger of physical abuse.

A few children try to deal with their anger by acting in an acceptable way most of the time, so that parents and teachers assume that they are well-adjusted. When these children are frustrated, though, their hidden anger boils to the surface. They have tantrums and even self-destructive fits. During these fits, they may cut themselves with sharp objects, bang their heads against a hard surface, or find other ways to turn their rage on themselves.

When Rayetta was younger, it seemed as though many things upset her. If she misplaced one of her comic books and couldn't find it or if she made a mistake on her schoolwork, tears of anger would leak from her eyes. She hated herself for being such a "bad girl." As soon as she could, she would sneak away to a private place and start cussing herself. Within a short time, the rage would build so strong that she couldn't resist the urge to punish herself for being so terrible. Rayetta would sink her teeth into her forearm and bite herself as hard as she could. Sometimes she'd even draw blood. Afterward, when she had calmed down, she was always careful to hide her self-inflicted wounds from her mother.

Although children who have endured trauma don't usually suffer from flashbacks, intrusive thoughts, disassociation, or emotional numbing when the crisis was a one-time event, they *do* develop these symptoms if the trauma was ongoing. When disasters start piling up, children develop the ability to deny reality as they brace for shocks, according to Terr: "In an attempt to see no evil, hear no evil, speak no evil, and feel nothing, the youngster starts ignoring what is at hand. His senses go numb and he guards against thinking." Repeatedly abused children who become emotionally numb usually develop one of two personality styles: Some withdraw; others seem to be very sociable and charming around whomever they are with at the time, but they make no deep or lasting connections with other people.

Memory plays tricks on children who have been traumatized over and over again. They may report seeing things that aren't really there. Sometimes they remember the event differently than it really happened. Sense of time often becomes distorted in children who have disassociated, so that something that took several hours to happen seems to have passed in a minute. An event that went by in an instant may seem to have dragged on for hours. Children who have distorted memories of a trauma aren't making those memories up—they really believe what they are saying. These memories reflect an inner reality rather than reality in the outside world.

Sometimes, when adults hear a child's inaccurate stories about a traumatic event, they may disbelieve that the event ever happened to the child. Other times a child may accuse the wrong person of sexually abusing him or her without meaning to. As a result of several day-care scandals in which children accused caretakers of victimizing them in sexual satanic rituals, some law-enforcement officials and mental-health workers wonder whether children are capable of having *false memories,* memories about something that never happened to them at all. In some cases, social workers examining children for sexual abuse may plant the seeds of false memory in a child's mind by asking leading questions like "Where did the baby-sitter touch you?" instead of questions more likely to get at the truth, like, "Did the baby-sitter touch you?" In an attempt to please the adult, a child may provide the answers he or she thinks the questioner wants to hear.

While it is possible that children can transform some-thing that occurred to another person, something they have heard about, into a memory, or an event that was suggested to them into a trauma memory, Terr and many other researchers caution that most of the time children's memories are an expression of the child's inner reality. These memories need to be taken seriously, especially if a child displays symptoms of PTSD. A shocking number of children are abused. At the same time, we need to remember that the details in children's trauma memories aren't always 100 percent accurate.

When Rayetta was little, she told her mother a boogie man came into her room at night, a big monster with fangs for teeth and a sharp tail. He'd poke her with the tail, she said. Her mother thought she was making the story up. "You have an overactive imagination," she told her daughter. She told other people that Rayetta was too high-strung and ignored her daughter's story. Eventu-ally, Rayetta ignored the reality of her sexual abuse as well. After her mother broke up with her boyfriend and Rayetta was safe, she altogether put what had happened to her out of her mind. Only when Paul began flirting with her did the old memories begin to rise to the surface in the form of dreams. Even though they started to come back into her awareness, she still wasn't certain what was causing them.

Some children and young people who have endured repeated trauma do manage to forget completely what has happened to them, suppressing the memory deep in their subconscious, as Rayetta did. Their ability to split off from their emotions and physical sensations as well as their ability to "forget" what occurred are coping strategies that help them to survive the continuing trauma when there is no way to end it. In effect, it is an escape hatch. Once the abuse stops on its own or the children are old enough to force it to end, the memories may remain buried until they are later triggered by an event that reminds the person of the trauma.

5

When a Parent Has PTSD

Carlos and his little sister spend most of their time trying to avoid their father's anger. They both love their dad, but they're afraid of him, too, because there's no way of telling when or at what he'll blow his top next. Even when he tries to show his love for them by taking them on an outing to the mountains or a lake, something always seems to set him off. The drivers in front of them are too slow, the restaurant doesn't cook the hamburgers right, or Carlos and his sister make too much noise. Most of the time it's easier to stay at home.

Carlos's mother tries to keep peace in the family but cries quite a bit lately and always seems tired. Carlos feels as if nothing he can ever do will please his dad—lately, he's stopped trying. He counts the days until he's old enough to leave home for good, and he's promised himself that he will *never* treat his children the way his dad has treated him.

When a parent has survived a traumatic event and suffers from PTSD, everyone in the family is affected by the parent's symptoms. They become secondary victims of whatever trauma the parent experienced. For example, a 1985 study of Vietnam veterans by Rosenheck and Nathan found that sons and daughters of combat veterans showed stress reactions similar to those of their fathers. At least two studies of combat veterans, one in the United States and one in Israel, have shown that soldiers whose fathers suffered from combat-related PTSD are more vulnerable to suffering from the same disorder themselves after they experience a combat situation.

If a parent's PTSD goes untreated for a long period of time, then the chances of his or her spouse and children becoming traumatized during the course of living with the post-traumatic stress disorder in the household grow higher. When Carlos's father pushed his little girl down the stairs in order to save her from an imagined enemy attack, she became a primary victim of trauma—the trauma of being physically hurt by her father. She is also a secondary victim of combat trauma from the Vietnam War.

Carlos has been hurt by his father, but his wounds are emotional rather than physical. Because his dad is often short-tempered and always on the lookout for the enemy, Carlos is jumpy and has a hard time sleeping. The primary trauma that Carlos has faced ever since his birth is that of growing up with an unpredictable and frequently angry father.

Any severe emotional shock can affect how a person relates to others. Some of the more common traumatic experiences a parent might have faced in childhood or as a young adult and that may affect how they act today, including the way they raise their children, are:

- Incest
- Child abuse

- Their parent's alcoholism or drug abuse
- Chronic illness
- Combat

In families like the one in which Carlos lives, one of the parents has had PTSD since before the children were born. The disorder is long-term, or what psychologists call *chronic.* Often the parent's post-traumatic stress disorder has never been diagnosed or treated. In many cases the other parent has developed PTSD over time from loving and living with a trauma victim and from trying to raise a family in a troubled atmosphere.

Partners of people with chronic PTSD quite frequently find that most of their time is taken up dealing with the problems of the person who has been traumatized so long ago. Sometimes they have little time left over to be attentive parents. They may, like Carlos's mom, have little energy as well. When they are feeling stressed or temporarily depressed, their spouse is unable to give them help or comfort because their spouse's life is so controlled by PTSD.

Because the growing awareness that PTSD affects whole families is so new, little research has been done on families of people with PTSD. As of the time of this writing, no major studies have been conducted specifically on their children. In one 1988 study, when asked to fill out a questionnaire about the ways they saw PTSD affecting combat veterans' families, counselors at Vet Centers answered that the most common problems reported to them by wives and girlfriends were:

- Coping with the partner's emotional numbing
- Coping with the partner's hypersensitivity
- Loneliness and lack of a social life
- Coping with the partner's verbal abuse
- Fear of speaking to the partner
- Self-doubts
- Constantly responding to the partner's needs

- Coping with the partner's angry outbursts.

Even though children's opinions weren't gathered, it is safe to assume that they, too, face many of the problems as partners of combat veterans.

Not all parents who have PTSD developed it before they began raising their own families. Some are hit with major emotional shocks at a time in life when their children are old enough to be aware of what has happened. Their kids can remember how their parents acted before the trauma and are now confronted with a rapid change in behavior that can be quite an upset. Often they feel frightened for their parent, scared that something even worse than the trauma will happen and that it will hurt their parent even more.

Events that can suddenly cause PTSD and affect the way a parent acts toward his or her children are:

- Rape
- Violent crime
- Domestic violence
- Accidents
- A death in the family
- Divorce

Professional interest in learning how PTSD affects whole families is slowly growing. Recently some V.A. hospitals have begun to offer family therapy, including both children and spouses as part of their PTSD programs that serve veterans. Mental-health workers who treat adults who were incest victims have begun offering therapy to their partners. Adults who grew up in alcoholic families have banded together to start their own self-help support groups in order to heal from their traumas. In all probability this trend will continue.

In the past, therapists saw many people who had lingering problems from growing up with a parent's PTSD. These parents had endured many kinds of trauma, but usually that subject wasn't brought up during the adult child's therapy. Remember that PTSD wasn't recognized as an emotional disorder and didn't even have a name until 15 years ago. The information therapists learned from talking to their clients about how a parent's PTSD affects his or her family wasn't collected or systematically recorded. In the future more attention will be paid to the studying and meeting the needs of children whose parents have suffered from traumatic events.

A Family Secret

When a school counselor called Rayetta into her office because of her difficulties in concentrating in the classroom, Rayetta shared her confusion and concerns. The counselor suggested that Rayetta's mom come in so that the three of them could discuss the problem. During that appointment, the counselor told Rayetta's mother that her daughter's dreams and reaction to Paul could be indications of childhood sexual abuse or incest. At first Rayetta's mother denied that anything of the sort could have happened, but then she admitted that during her relationship, her boyfriend had watched her daughter while she worked nights.

"I didn't think it at the time, but maybe something could have gone on." Her words were hesitant. "I did hear, after I broke up with him, that he'd been fooling around with one of his sister's little girls, touching her. From what I heard, he went to prison for it, but I didn't think he'd done anything nasty to Rayetta. Even if he had, as long as I didn't bring it up, I knew she'd forget it in time."

She stopped for a minute and shredded a tissue crumpled on her lap. "My grandfather did something to me when I was a girl, but I forgot about it and didn't let it get to me. It wasn't any big deal." Cautiously she looked at her daughter. "There's no use crying over spilled milk."

Rayetta sat bolt upright in her chair and stared at her mother in disbelief and outrage. How could she have known about her former boyfriend and never said anything? How could she sit here now and act as if her own daughter being molested years ago wasn't important? Before Rayetta could confront her, her mother began sobbing. "I guess I didn't forget about it, did I? I guess it *was* a big deal. After all these years it hurts so much." She reached over and hugged Rayetta. "And now you're hurting, baby." Her avoidance symptoms had caused Rayetta's mother to deny all the clues that her daughter was being molested, even to the point of becoming angry at her when she told on her mother's boyfriend so many years ago.

Even today a parent's post-traumatic stress disorder can remain a secret, unless someone like Rayetta's school counselor uncovers it, sometimes by accident.

Therapists who treat victims of incest have found that parents who suffered from physical abuse or sexual molestation as children sometimes avoided thinking about the past. Some try to deny that long-ago trauma so much that they ignore those same traumas when they happen to their own children, such as Rayetta's mother did.

In addition, counselors who have worked with child abusers and perpetrators of incest have also noticed that quite frequently their clients were abused or molested when they were children. Many times this abuse was kept a secret for years and was untreated. The person who was physically or sexually abused as a child attempted to cope with the emotional shock of that extreme stress by identifying with the abuser. After that person grew up and had children, he or she acted out their pasts on their own offspring.

From these observations, mental-health professionals have concluded that the problems of child abuse and incest, which tend to cause chronic PTSD in their victims, if kept secret and untreated, can be passed along from generation to generation. For this reason they are called *intergenera-tional* problems.

How a Parent's PTSD
Affects Children

Young people like Carlos and Rayetta who grow up in families in which someone has chronic PTSD often don't know what it is like to be raised by a parent without PTSD because they have never had that opportunity. They may come to accept the intrusive thoughts, avoidance symptoms, and hyperalertness they often see in both parents as a normal way of life. As these children grow older, they sometimes have a feeling that something is wrong with their parent and in their family, but often they aren't quite sure what it is.

Whether a parent's post-traumatic stress disorder has been long-term or is fairly recent, their PTSD can affect their children in many ways. It is important to know that not all children are affected in the same way. One reason for this is that, as we learned earlier, not all parents who suffer from post-traumatic stress disorder have it to the same extent. Their symptoms may vary from those other people have after experiencing the same trauma. For example, some combat veterans become violent when they are angry, but 50 percent of them do not. Some are so troubled by their PTSD symptoms that they cannot hold a job. Others are quite successful and manage to hide their PTSD symptoms. They may be cold and distant to their children, but never raise their voices to them in anger.

The experiences of children differ as well. One child in a family can be affected to a great extent from a parent's PTSD while a brother or sister may hardly be affected at all. The relationship between each brother and sister and the parent is a different one. Some children may also have coping skills in the face of stress that work better than those of their brothers and sisters.

The following list includes some of the feelings children and young adults who live with someone who has PTSD have. As you read it, ask yourself if you have ever felt any similar feelings.

Children living with a parent who has PTSD sometimes:

- Grow up with a sense of shame, especially when the parent's trauma has been kept a secret from them
- Feel angry at what- or whomever caused the trauma if they know what happened to their parent, but feel helpless to do anything about it
- Feel angry at their parent and then feel guilty for feeling angry
- Resent having their lives controlled by a parent's trauma, something that didn't happen to them and isn't their fault
- Sometimes feel invisible because the parent's problems always seem to take center stage
- Feel neglected because they often don't get their emotional needs met
- Have low self-worth from accepting blame for causing a parent's symptoms
- Are exhausted from trying to take care of their parent's emotional and physical needs
- Feel jumpy and nervous much of the time, but aren't sure about the cause of their anxiety

Living with PTSD is no fun, even when you aren't the one with the disorder. The specific symptoms of PTSD that make life so difficult for some trauma victims can make their children's lives difficult as well. Take a few moments to review the symptoms of PTSD and imagine what kind of effect each symptom would have on your ability to love and nurture a child.

Intrusive Symptoms

Obsessive thoughts, nightmares, and flashbacks often cause a parent's attention to be far away from the family. It is as if that person is stuck in the past and unable to live or love or have feelings in the moment. A parent with PTSD may be physically present, but their thoughts and feelings are stuck in another time and place. When a child tries to talk with a parent struggling with intrusive symptoms, that child may be brushed aside or otherwise ignored.

The fear, grief, and rage that are often triggered by dreams and flashbacks don't always make sense to someone who hasn't been through the trauma and doesn't share memories of that trauma with the victim. When Carlos's dad blows up at his son for making too much noise, he's reacting to something that happened years ago. In the jungles of Vietnam, soldiers who made too much noise attracted the enemy, putting their own lives and the lives of their fellow soldiers at risk. His dad's rage is bewildering and frightening to Carlos. He blames himself for causing his father's feelings and his temper tantrums.

Rayetta's mom's fury at her young daughter several years ago, when the girl told on her mom's boyfriend, was triggered by Rayetta's speaking out, but the actual anger came from her own childhood experiences. She was still angry at herself for not stopping the incest that happened to her, and she felt guilty about being victimized, mistakenly blaming herself. Because she hadn't openly acknowledged her feelings and tried to work through them, Rayetta's mother couldn't help her daughter when she most needed help. Instead she vented the self-hatred and shame she had been storing up for a lifetime on her daughter. Rayetta, not having any idea of the real source of her mom's feelings, became infected by that self-hatred and shame, making them her own.

Even though Carlos's noisemaking and the fact that Rayetta had been molested as a little girl served as triggers for their parents' intrusive symptoms, those symptoms weren't Carlos's and Rayetta's fault. They did not deserve to become the targets of their parents' extreme and negative emotions. Neither did they deserve to be blamed for the outbursts. In an attempt to avoid thinking about the trauma, people with PTSD often blame the trigger instead of the trauma itself for their bad feelings. When kids don't know this, it's difficult for them *not* to take responsibility for how their parent is feeling and acting during a flashback or after a bad dream.

Because parents with PTSD have little or no control over when intrusive symptoms will arise, they often feel as though their lives are completely out of their control. The lives of the people they live with seem out of control as well. Many times it is impossible for a child to predict how a parent with PTSD will act at any given time or in any given situation. For this reason children whose parents have PTSD often find it hard to trust their parents and the world around them—they never know what will happen next.

They may resent that most of their time and energy is spent going from crisis to crisis, provoked by a parent's intrusive PTSD symptoms. Sometimes it may appear as if the whole family spends all of its time taking care of the parent with PTSD—calming them down, making excuses to others for their behavior, doing the day-to-day jobs around the house that the person with PTSD can't handle because they are too emotionally troubled to do them.

Avoidance Symptoms

Because a parent with PTSD tries to avoid anything that will remind him or her of the original trauma, the whole family may avoid many activities that other families enjoy. The Fourth of July, a time when most people are celebrating, is one of the worst times of the year for Carlos and his family.

A parent with PTSD may feel uncomfortable being among people and refuse to go places where there may be crowds. One who has survived a bad automobile accident might refuse to drive anymore, putting an end to a child's afterschool activities. Potential triggers that are avoided can range from minor to major ones, and children who grow up with a PTSD-plagued parent may constantly try to keep his or her parent protected from reminders of what happened so long ago. For Carlos this often feels like he's walking across a field of hidden landmines. If he takes one step in the wrong direction, his dad will explode.

As we mentioned earlier, people with PTSD often blame others for triggering their intrusive symptoms and the storm of uncomfortable emotions that accompany them. Many times they blame their families, including their children, for all their other troubles that are caused by avoidance. Carlos's dad says he could keep a job longer if his wife just didn't nag him. He claims he keeps moving the family from house to house because she's never happy with where they live. The fact that he quits his work and moves so often is all her fault, he says. The war has nothing to do with it.

Sometimes the whole family tries to avoid thinking about the original trauma that started causing their loved one so many problems. Not only do family members accept the blame for a parent's or partner's PTSD symptoms, but they may deny that anything is wrong with the parent or the family. The trauma often becomes a shameful family secret because of this tendency to avoid and deny the real problem. Carlos's dad won't talk about many of his experiences during the Vietnam War with anyone. Nobody in the family ever questions him out of fear their questions will make him upset. A parent's refusal to talk about what happened so long ago, and a family's refusal to acknowledge why that parent is so difficult to live with, causes kids to feel shame. And sometimes they have no idea what they feel so ashamed of. They sense that their family is different, but they aren't sure why.

Parents with PTSD use psychic numbing to avoid thoughts or memories of their original traumas. Often they feel cold and distant from everyone, especially their partners and children. Rayetta's mother was always busy. Even when she didn't have to work, she made her boyfriend primarily responsible for taking care of the little girl when she wasn't in day care. Today Rayetta can remember only a few occasions when her mom ever hugged her or played with her. Instead, she always seemed to be pushing her away. Carlos's dad has never told him that he loves him. He doesn't ask about how Carlos is doing in school and doesn't seem to care about anybody else's feelings but his own. It is no wonder that Carlos has such problems feeling good about himself.

Parents with PTSD don't deliberately set out to emotionally hurt their children, but often their problems get in the way of providing those children with the emotional support and closeness that they need. As a result, children whose parents have PTSD may feel unloved. In time they may come to believe that they are not worthy of being loved. Their shame about being part of a family with a secret is intensified because they feel unworthy of being loved by anyone.

Hyperarousal Symptoms

When a parent with PTSD is on edge all or most of the time, the people they live with tend to be anxious as well. Sometimes the edginess comes out in the form of being overprotective. A parent who witnessed or was involved in a fatal car crash might be reluctant to let his or her kids ride in a car and later may forbid them to get a driver's license. A mother who has been raped may be so frightened for her daughter when she begins dating that she forbids her daughter to have a social life. A father whose brother committed suicide as a teenager might get nervous every time one of his kids is alone in their room. He might make a rule that the doors to their rooms must be open and check up on them frequently, violating their need for privacy. Overprotectiveness like the examples discussed above, causes both children and young adults to be resentful.

People who are frequently jumpy and irritable because they have PTSD often don't like to be around other people. They may isolate themselves in an attempt to keep calmer. Often their families become isolated, too. Carlos, when he was younger, could never have friends over to play at his house. Now that he's older, he doesn't even ask his parents if other kids can come over. He would be too embarrassed to have them witness his father's unpredictable outbursts. Carlos's mother has few friends because all of her time is taken up by Carlos's dad. Aunts, uncles, and grandparents from both sides of the family have stopped visiting because Carlos's dad never seemed happy to see them.

The loneliness that comes from isolation only adds to the self-blame and shame that children often feel when a parent has PTSD. Their isolation sometimes makes them feel that their mother or father is the only person in the world who acts this way and that their family is the only one struggling with the problems caused by trauma. Only when they realize they are not alone can they reach out for help.

6

Recovering from PTSD

After her talk with the school counselor, Rayetta felt as though a big weight had been lifted from her shoulders, one she had been carrying around for years. Even so, she knew she had a lot of work to do on herself before she could get rid of her fears and begin to live her life in the way she wanted to. She also knew she needed help to do it. On her own, she didn't have the slightest idea of how to begin. The school counselor gave Rayetta and her mother a referral to Ms. Davis, a psychologist at the county mental-health clinic who specialized in working with incest survivors.

Rayetta and her mother attended the first appointment together. Beforehand Rayetta's mom told her daughter that she wanted to get her the help she needed but that she didn't need any help for herself, not from a psychologist. Ms. Davis seemed to understand what Rayetta told her and how she felt, so that it was easy to talk to her. Even Rayetta's mother talked. At the end of the session, Ms.

Davis suggested that Rayetta come back to see her on a weekly basis. She told Rayetta's mother that she would like to begin individual therapy with her as well and gave her the phone numbers of two incest-survivor support groups that she might benefit from attending. Later they might begin family therapy.

Over the next few months Rayetta saw Ms. Davis once a week. A little bit at a time she began to feel better about herself and to understand what had happened to her as well as how it had changed her life. She still had difficult times, but more and more now she felt she was gaining control over how she felt and the choices she made. Even though Rayetta's mother didn't go back to see Ms. Davis or attend the support groups, she supported her daughter's healing and thinks that someday she might go to a group meeting. She's just not ready yet.

Carlos's father was discharged from the army 25 years ago. In all that time, he hasn't tried to get help for his PTSD. Some of his buddies attend groups at the Vet Center. Others have gone through the six-week PTSD program offered at the local V.A. hospital, where they spend the whole time working through their memories of and reactions to the Vietnam War.

Whenever Carlos's mom used to bring up the idea that it might be a good idea for his dad to see a therapist at the V.A. hospital, his dad would always get mad. He said that the problem wasn't his fault—she and the children were to blame for the way he felt and acted. He argued that, even if he had a problem, he'd rather put a gun to his head and blow out his brains than see a shrink at the V.A.

Afraid that his father would eventually carry out his threat, Carlos called a crisis hotline one night. The man who answered the phone listened patiently to all the fear and rage that Carlos had been storing up for years. All his life he'd been hurt by a war that was over before he was born, he stormed. It wasn't fair. When Carlos admitted that there were times he'd thought of taking his own life because it seemed as though nothing he ever did was good enough for his dad, the telephone crisis counselor calmed him down. Then he gave Carlos the name and address of a local youth crisis center with counselors. Maybe they could help him to find positive ways to cope with the constant turmoil of life with a former combat vet.

During his first counseling session, Carlos was given the number for the local V.A. Hospital. His new counselor suggested that he get into a therapy group for children of veteran's with PTSD. It wasn't that simple. The people at the V.A. said that they wouldn't help family members unless the veteran himself was receiving some kind of treatment and to try the Vet Center. Ready to give up, Carlos called the number for the Vet Center, an outreach program for veterans and their families. They had no formal counseling programs for teenagers, but the counselor there told Carlos he'd be glad to talk with him about the PTSD and educate him about how it affected families of veterans. Maybe, together, they could find some answers for Carlos.

According to Dr. Judith Lewis Herman, author of *Trauma and Recovery,* freedom from PTSD is most effectively accomplished when the person who has undergone a traumatic event forms a healing relationship with a helping professional and finds a safe place to talk about the trauma. Remembering what happened and mourning the losses must occur before reconnecting with the world and with others. Ultimately PTSD sufferers must grapple with the question "Why me?" and search for the positive gifts that enduring trauma has brought into their lives. Rayetta and Carlos are beginning to do just that.

Many people who have endured a traumatic event and suffer from post-traumatic stress disorder avoid getting help like Rayetta's mother and Carlos's dad. Many people who have been traumatized don't want to think about what has happened to them. They know that in order to get the help they need, they will *have* to think and talk about the trauma, and they are afraid of setting off another round of intrusive symptoms. Because the avoidance symptoms of PTSD can also cause people to blame anything but the trauma itself for their problems, they may not believe that anything is wrong with them. It is the rest of the world that is messed up.

When people with PTSD have suffered from secondary victimization because other people tried to blame them for the traumatic event, they may be reluctant to talk about what occurred—even to a therapist. They expect they will be blamed, shamed, or made to feel guilty about something that wasn't their fault. Other reasons that some people with PTSD decide not to get help include:

- Fear that they are crazy or stupid, and that instead of helping them, therapy will only make them feel worse about themselves
- Feeling that if they don't talk about the past and keep it well-hidden that eventually they will forget what happened
- Believing that, since the trauma, everything is out of their control and that they are so helpless that nothing can make their lives better
- Feeling that they ought to be tough enough to handle the aftereffects of trauma by themselves

Finding Help

"Healing from trauma is something no one should have to go through alone. Indeed, in many cases doing so is almost impossible, and virtually any trauma survivor can benefit from the right kind of help," advises Dr. Aphrodite Matsakis in *I Can't Get Over It: A Handbook for Trauma Survivors*. Matsakis defines the right kind of help as high-quality help that is suited to the individual.

Because people with post-traumatic stress disorder have such a difficult time connecting with other people, it is very important that they find *good* helpers to help them make their desire for healing a reality.   Good helpers, whether they are friends, family members, self-help group members, or professional therapists:

- Listen with compassion when the person with PTSD expresses his or her feelings.
- Respect that person's feelings.
- Offer reassurance and support, not pity.
- Don't try to tell the trauma victim what they should or shouldn't have done or be feeling.
- Recognize that the trauma caused the PTSD and don't criticize or blame trauma survivors.
- Understand that PTSD isn't caused by character weakness
- Acknowledge that traumatic events can have a major impact on people who experience them.
- Validate trauma victims instead of hinting that they have made up the trauma or are talking about it just to get attention.

Sometimes these helpers are close friends or family members. Even though they haven't received professional training about how to help PTSD victims, they are willing to listen and to lend a hand. The support they provide is very important to the healing process. Even Carlos, in the middle of his resentment, still loves his dad. He wants his father to stop suffering and would do anything within his power to help him.

Have you ever been in a situation where someone needed your help and you paid so much attention to them that you forgot about taking care of your own needs? Maybe you spent so much time with that person that you didn't have a minute in the day to do what you wanted to do. Perhaps you became so caught up in their problems that you began to feel worse than they did. Friends and family members who try to help someone with post-traumatic stress disorder often find themselves in this position, especially if they live with the trauma victim. They get so caught up in the other person's PTSD that they burn out.

When you are helping or living with someone who has PTSD, you need to take care of yourself as well. It is important for you to:

- Maintain a life of your own; avoid becoming a full-time crisis manager.
- Keep friendships with other people instead of isolating and focusing all of your attention on the person with PTSD.
- Understand that a person with PTSD may have very little to give in a relationship and reach out for emotional support for *yourself* from other sources, such as therapy or self-help groups, when you need it.
- Learn to nurture yourself by paying attention to your own needs and taking time for yourself.
- Avoid feeling survivor guilt. Trauma happens. Often it has happened randomly. It isn't your fault that it happened to your friend or relative instead of you. Neither is it your fault that you can't make the trauma victim feel better. People can't fix other people. Often the best you can do is to be there for your friend or family member and to listen. That is good enough.

Even when friends and family members can't be or don't know how to be supportive, help for PTSD can come in the form of a concerned teacher or school counselor, as it did for Rayetta. Her counselor was able to refer her to yet another form of helper, a psychologist who specialized in working with incest victims. Weekly or twice-weekly therapy with a counselor who has experience and training in treating survivors of trauma is one of the most common ways of healing from the lingering aftereffects of severe emotional shock. Usually these hour-long therapy sessions last a few weeks or months. When the PTSD has gone untreated for a long time or when a traumatic event stirs up another, earlier trauma that hasn't been worked through, individual therapy tends to take longer. The longer you wait, the longer it will take for you to recover, advises Mariann Hybels-Steer, Ph.D. a Los Angeles psychologist and author of *Aftermath: Survive and Overcome Trauma.*

When the person with PTSD is ready, his or her therapist may suggest moving from individual to group therapy. Here, under the guidance of a psychologist, psychiatrist, or counselor, several people meet to discuss the effect of a particular trauma on their lives. In addition to providing emotional support, therapy groups allow people with PTSD to learn to relate to others in a healthy way. Because such groups are led by a professional, there is usually a fee involved. Sometimes the fee charged is based on the client's income.

Not all therapists are alike. Not only do they use different styles of treatment, they have different personalities. In order for the healing relationship to work effectively, a client needs to respect and trust the professional they have chosen to help them. Because working with the wrong therapist can cause secondary trauma, it is important for a person with PTSD to find out if the therapist has training in treating PTSD, how long that person has been working with trauma survivors, and how many trauma survivors he or she has treated.

A more intense type of help than individual or group therapy is offered in PTSD treatment programs, like the one some of Carlos's dad's friends have attended at the V.A. hospital. Treatment programs are usually residential; the person healing from PTSD spends all day in individual and group counseling sessions, as well as participating in other activities designed to help work through the trauma and raise self-esteem. Instead of going home in the evening, the treatment program patient stays at the hospital or treatment center. Because getting better is the only thing he or she must focus on, clients at treatment programs are often able to make major changes in a matter of weeks.

The self-help support group that the counselor suggested Rayetta's mother attend offers yet a different kind of help—the insights and encouragement from people who have been through the same experience. Although a self-help group may have a leader, that person isn't a professional counselor. Having survived the trauma is the leader's qualification for running a self-help-group meeting. Often group members share the leadership role. Members of self-help groups often assist one another by trading information about good therapists and treatment programs. Quite frequently, they form friendships that extend outside of the weekly meetings. Sometimes support groups become politically active, advocating for prevention and victim's rights. Most self-help groups are free of charge.

Even though Carlos isn't getting therapy from the Vet Center, and he hasn't yet hooked up with a self-help group, he is learning about his father's emotional problems and how they have changed the whole family. By becoming educated about PTSD, he is slowly discovering how important it is for him stop accepting the blame for his father's emotional suffering and to start taking better care of himself.

Some people who have PTSD either can't find another person to talk with or they aren't ready to talk about what has happened to them. Education about PTSD can also come in the form of books like this one, TV shows, and movies. Even though learning about PTSD can't take the place of therapy, it does provide a starting point for healing.

Several sources of help are listed at the end of this book. Many of these resources can refer you to therapists and self-help groups in your area. In addition to these resources, you can try the following places for a referral for help for a particular trauma:

- Hospitals
- Mental-health clinics

- Community mental health associations
- Government social service agencies
- Statewide professional associations, such as psychological associations or psychiatric associations

Crisis hotlines and other sources of assistance, such as battered women's shelters, rape crisis counseling services, and victim's assistance programs are usually listed in the telephone book. If you can't find them in the White Pages, try looking in the Yellow Pages under the headings: *Social Service Organizations, Support Groups,* or *Mental Health Services.* Another good strategy is to look for a heading for the specific problem, such as *Suicide Prevention* or *Child Abuse Services.*   Often your local library will have this information as well, or the reference librarian can point you in the right direction to find it.

Healing from PTSD

No matter what recovery method a trauma survivor chooses, experts who work with people who suffer with the aftermath of emotional shock note that there are many stages in the healing process. At each step the person with PTSD has special needs that must be met if healing is to take place.

Before a trauma survivor can really begin emotional healing, he or she needs to find safety. Usually that involves getting away from the physically dangerous environment. Soldiers who develop acute combat stress reactions must be shipped from the battlefield in order to recover. A battered woman has to leave her abusive spouse, perhaps moving herself and her children to a safe house or a shelter, before she can think about her emotional scars. A child who is physically or sexually abused must be protected from the possibility of revictimization, sometimes being removed from the family, before he or she is able to heal.

Sometimes finding safety involves getting medical treatment, as Bill did in the emergency room. It may mean contacting law-enforcement officials to report a rape or violent crime and then getting legal help either through a private attorney or a victims' assistance program set up to ensure the rights of people who have been victimized.

Trauma victims also need to be emotionally safe. That means telling their stories to people they can trust, not people who either make negative judgments against them or refuse to listen at all. Because Karen's mom brushes her daughter off when she expresses her feelings about the apartment fire, Karen doesn't feel safe sharing her emotions with her mom. Right after the fire, the kids at school were curious and asked a number of questions, but what had happened to Karen quickly became old news and they acted bored when she tried talking about it. Unable to tell anyone about what had happened and what it has meant to her, for months she couldn't move beyond the PTSD symptoms that had begun to control her life.

Recently, though, Karen watched a made-for-TV movie about a family whose house burned down. Seeing the problems the fictional family members faced after their tragedy, she felt a little less alone. Lately she has been able to open up a little bit at a time about her feelings in letters to an aunt who lives across the country. She feels safe writing to her aunt because her aunt doesn't give Karen advice; she just listens. Each time Karen writes some more about what happened to her, she feels a little better, as though the secret burden of pain and fear is going away, one small piece at a time.

Reducing intrusive thoughts, flashbacks, and nightmares about a trauma and the physical arousal symptoms that accompany them is the next task the person with PTSD and his or her therapist must face. As we learned in Chapter Two, extreme stress triggers powerful responses in the bodies of those who endure traumatic events, responses like raised blood pressure and muscle tension. When people develop PTSD, those physical reactions continue long after the stress is gone. Some people with PTSD resort to alcohol or drugs in order to try to calm themselves. Hyperarousal, feeling jumpy and on guard most of the time, uses up so much of their energy that people with PTSD often don't feel they have the physical or emotional strength to begin remembering and talking about the trauma during therapy.

For this reason, some psychotherapists encourage their PTSD clients to learn to manage their body's responses to hyperarousal through diet, exercise, and other stress-reducing activities, such as meditation. Once the hyperarousal symptoms have been lessened, people have an easier time in their daily activities and they are better able to cope with the difficult task of remembering what happened that emotional healing requires.

Some people with PTSD aren't able to diminish their hyperarousal symptoms using the abovementioned means. No matter what they do, they still can't concentrate or sleep at night. Often when this is the case, people who struggle with a long-term physical reaction to stress are prescribed mood-altering drugs in an attempt to restore the brain's neurochemistry to balance.

According to Jonathan Davidson, associate professor of the department of psychiatry at Duke University Medical Center, the six reasons for using drugs to treat PTSD are to:

- Reduce intrusive symptoms, including nightmares, flash-backs, and uncontrollable thoughts about the trauma
- Improve avoidance symptoms, including emotional numbing and staying away from activities that might trigger memories of trauma
- Lessen long-term hyperarousal, the body's fight-or-flight response, that can cause sleeplessness and constantly being on guard against something bad that might happen
- Relieve depression

- Help the PTSD patient to control his or her impulses
- Control severe disassociation

Some of the mood-altering, or psychiatric, drugs that are commonly used to treat post-traumatic stress disorder are: tricyclic drugs (antidepressants), monoamine oxidase inhibitors, carbmazepine, beta-blockers, lithium, and benzodiazepines (tranquilizers such as Valium).

Bill finally asked his mother to make an appointment for him with the family doctor so he could get a prescription for something to help him to sleep at night. If he could just get some rest, he thought, he'd be able to concentrate once again and pull his grades up. Bill's doctor was concerned about the dark circles under his young patient's eyes and his obvious exhaustion, but he was cautious about prescribing sedative sleeping pills for Bill. Instead, he suggested that Bill see a psychiatrist. The psychiatrist might decide that Bill needed medication after talking with him, but maybe therapy alone would take care of Bill's sleeplessness.

After evaluating Bill, the psychiatrist prescribed a mild antidepressant, but told him that there was no magic pill to cure PTSD. The medication would allow him to function a little better at home and at school and, hopefully, it would let him get some sleep. In the meantime, Bill would need to come to weekly therapy sessions in order to talk through the emotions being mugged had stirred in him. After a few weeks of therapy, he would be able to get back to living his life without medication.

Most other professionals who treat PTSD believe that mood-altering drugs should always be used in combination with psychotherapy. Used alone, drugs don't solve the problem of post-traumatic stress disorder; they simply make life a little easier for people who have been through traumatic events by decreasing their symptoms. The most recent research on using drugs to help treat PTSD indicates that tricyclic antidepressants are currently considered the most effective drugs and that, in order to work, they must be taken for at least eight weeks. Most psychiatrists, like Bill's, constantly monitor how their patient is doing on the prescribed drug and stop the drug therapy as soon as the PTSD sufferer finds enough emotional balance through treatment to continue without mood-altering drugs.

Once hyperarousal is under control, a person with PTSD can begin regaining a reasonable degree of control over the daily events of life. Because traumatic stress often leaves people feeling helpless, they may withdraw from the activities of daily life, believing they no longer have any say in what happens to them. Carlos felt that way until he called the crisis hotline. With that one small step, he began taking charge of his life again. The first steps to gaining some control over life again after trauma can range from choosing a particular type of therapy to exercising control over events that have no close relationship to the trauma, events like deciding what movie to see with friends or cleaning out a closet.

Taking charge can also mean taking action to help prevent a similar trauma from happening in the future. For example, if Karen's mom won't buy a smoke detector for her room, Karen could take control by saving up her own money and buying one herself. Bill might want to enroll in a self-defense class to boost his confidence and physical strength. Rayetta could take a workshop on assertiveness training so she could learn how to sit down, friend-to-friend, with Paul and tell him to back off on the flirting. When people with PTSD begin to exert some control over their lives, their attitude toward life and toward themselves begins to change. With each small success comes a more positive outlook, as hopelessness changes to hope.

At the same time that people with post-traumatic stress disorder begin putting their lives back in order, they need to begin straightening out the jumble of feelings inside of themselves. They do this by telling the story of what has happened to them to nonjudgmental people. Sometimes trauma victims need to tell their stories over and over again before they can make sense of what has happened. As Karen found, sometimes family members and friends may start out by reacting with understanding, but in time they grow bored with hearing about what happened.

That's where therapists and self-help-group members come in. These helpers know and understand that it often takes time to fully remember the event, especially if the person disassociated at the time of the trauma, as many incest and child-abuse survivors did. They know, as well, that it takes time to grieve for the things that trauma takes away from us. Karen lost her cat, which had been a great source of comfort and affection. She also lost her ability to feel safe in her own home. Carlos feels like he lost his whole childhood because he couldn't relax and be happy. Instead, he always had to be careful not to get his dad mad at him. Take a few minutes to think about the things, in your opinion, trauma might have taken from Carlos's father and from Bill and Rayetta.

Given all the things that PTSD has stolen from trauma survivors, it is no wonder that many times they become mistrustful of caring about other people. This is especially true when the trauma was caused by other people, like the gang members who mugged Bill, the soldiers who shot at Carlos's father, or the boyfriend who sexually abused Rayetta. One of the most important and the most difficult parts of healing from post-traumatic stress disorder is to learn to trust others by repairing old emotional attachments and forming new ones. It's hard work *not* to withdraw from others after a trauma. Many of the symptoms of PTSD cause sufferers to push others away.

Often someone trying to heal from it must not only deal with the trauma but with guilt over how their anxiety, irritability, and avoidance have affected people they care about. Many times therapists or self-help-group members are the only people a trauma survivor can bring him- or herself to trust or to care about. That's a start.

During the first few sessions with his psychiatrist, Bill was too embarrassed to say much. Later, once he knew he could trust the man, he slowly began to talk. It wasn't until two months after he began therapy that he felt like he wanted to end his isolation. Reconnecting with his friends seemed too hard a task to do on his own. Everytime he got next to kids his own age, he felt anxious. Besides, his friends had teased him, and he didn't want to put up with that anymore. What if they teased him again? What if suddenly, out of the blue, somebody threw a punch at him? People had started avoiding him because he'd given them the cold shoulder first. Maybe none of them would want to have anything to do with him anymore.

Together Bill and his psychiatrist figured out how he could reach out to other people while meeting his needs for physical and emotional safety. Bill decided that his former best friend, Mark, would be easiest to talk with, but he felt uncomfortable having a face-to-face conversation with him. Instead, he called him and talked for a few minutes. He was surprised that Mark sounded happy to hear from him; he even asked Bill to go to a concert that weekend. That was too much, too soon for Bill. Even the thought of being in a crowd caused him to panic. Instead of the concert, he suggested that they get together and rent some videos on another night. Mark agreed. Even though Bill is taking his time, he is learning to trust and to take care of his emotional needs at the same time. Rayetta, Karen, and Carlos are each doing the same in their own way.

Happily Ever After?

The last task in healing from trauma is making sense out of what has happened. It is also the most difficult and takes the most time, often years. Trauma turns lives upside down. Survivors are left with the questions: *Why did this happen to me?* and *Why did I survive?* Because traumas are out-of-the-ordinary and often random experiences, most people who endure them never completely answer these questions. Their search for meaning is a lifelong process. This is why most professionals believe that post-traumatic stress disorder can be treated, but rarely, if ever, is it completely cured.

Once trauma survivors find safety, take charge of their lives, grieve their losses, and reconnect with others, however, their symptoms decrease, and in time appear only occasionally when they are faced with a period of major stress in their lives. No longer prisoners of the past, their hearts and minds are unchained from the memories of the horrible things that happened to them. Like Bill, Rayetta, Karen, and Carlos are starting to do, they live in the present, and look forward to tomorrow. Although they are changed forever by trauma, the experience has given them insights, understanding, and the opportunities to grow.

7

Where to Find Help

General PTSD Resources

Free from Fear
1400 Bayley Street, Unit 15A
Pickering, Ontario
Canada L1W 3R2
(905) 831-3877
This national self-help group's mission is to educate the public in order to remove the stigma that surrounds PTSD. They help to set up support groups and make referrals.

Institute for Victims of Trauma
6801 Market Square Drive
MacLean, VA 22101
(703) 847-8456
Lelia Dane, Ph.D., a clinical psychologist runs this organization, which helps victims of terrorism, accidents, natural and human-made disasters, and other traumatic events as well as their families and friends. The institute provides telephone counseling and referrals.

International Society for Traumatic Stress Studies
435 North Michigan Avenue, Suite 1717
Chicago, IL 60611-4067
(708) 480-9080
Members of this group include mental-health, education, social service, religious, research, and legal professionals. They publish a newsletter, *Traumatic Stress Points,* and *The Journal of Traumatic Stress,* a quarterly professional publication. They make referrals.

National Center for Post-Traumatic Stress Disorder
V.A. Medical Center 116D
White River Junction, VT 05009
(809) 296-5132
This resource center is a congressionally mandated clearinghouse for research, education, and training. Their resources include an extensive library and an electronic database.

Youth Crisis Hotline
(800) HIT-HOME
Privately funded by Youth Development International, this crisis line specializes in intervention counseling and referrals for people 18 and under. They deal with any kind of crisis, from homework to suicide.

Help for Specific Problems

Child Abuse/Domestic Violence

C. Henry Kempe National Center for the Prevention and
  Treatment of Child Abuse
1205 Oneida
Denver, CO 80220
(303) 321-3963

This center is made up of professionals. It provides information and referrals and actively works to stop child abuse.

National Clearinghouse on Childhood Abuse and Neglect
P.O. Box 1182
Washington, DC 20013
(800) 394-3366
This clearinghouse gathers and provides information on a variety of topics having to do with child abuse. They do not make referrals.

National Coalition Against Domestic Violence
P.O. Box 34103
Washington, DC 20043-4103
(202) 638-6388
This organization provides information about domestic violence and referrals to local shelters and mental-health professionals who work with victims of battering.

National Resource Center on Child Abuse and Neglect
63 Inverness Drive East
Englewood, CO 80112-5117
(800) 227-5242
This center, which is sponsored by the American Humane Association Children's Division, spreads information about child abuse and can make local referrals.

Women Helping Women
P.O. Box 552, Station U
Toronto, Ontario
Canada M8Z 5T8
(416) 252-7949
This organization provides information and referrals about all kinds of violent crimes that happen to women and

children, including domestic violence, rape, and child abuse.

Children of Chemically Dependent Parents

Adult Children of Alcoholics
6381 Hollywood Boulevard, Suite 685
Hollywood, CA 90028
(213) 464-4423
This organization is based on the Twelve Steps of Alcoholics Anonymous and focuses on recovery for both young people and adults who were raised by an alcoholic parent.

Al-Anon/Alateen Family Group
(800) 356-9996
Alanon and Alateen members work on their own recovery from living with an alcoholic. The organization provides a free information packet and can refer callers to local groups.

Al-Anon/Alateen Information Services
1712 Avenue Road
P.O. Box 54533
North York, Ontario
Canada M5M 4N5
(416) 366-4072
This group provides the same information and services as the U.S. group.

Canadian Association for Children of Alcoholics
555 University Avenue
Box 200
Toronto, Ontario
Canada M5G 1X8
(416) 813-5629
This group provides information and referrals for children of alcoholics throughout Canada.

Families Anonymous
(Families of Substance Abusers)
P.O. Box 528
Van Nuys, CA 91408
(818) 989-7841
Families Anonymous has more than 400 local chapters that help relatives and friends heal from the trauma that comes from loving someone who is chemically dependent.

Natural Disaster

American Red Cross
(Check your phone book for local listings.)
The Red Cross provides counseling for people who have experienced natural disasters. They also offer safety classes to help people prevent accidental trauma from happening.

Federal Emergency Management Agency
(800) 462-9029
This government agency helps to set up emergency counseling centers in disaster areas. They assist people who are victims of disasters by helping to provide funds for repairs and making referrals to crisis counselors.

Suicide

ALIVE Canada
1659 University Avenue West, Unit F
Windsor, Ontario
Canada N9B 1C3
(519) 252-9020
This group works for suicide prevention and awareness. They make referals as well.

Veterans and Their Families

VAMC Hospitals
Department of Veterans Affairs
941 North Capitol
Washington, DC 20421
(202) 265-6280

(Check your phone book for listings.)
Veterans Administration Medical Center hospitals offer PTSD treatment programs and counseling for veterans. Many also offer treatment programs and support groups for families of veterans who suffer from PTSD.

Vet Centers
National Veteran's Outreach Program
20 F Street NW
Washington, DC 20009
(202) 347-4885
(Check your phone book. These are sometimes listed as Readjustment Counseling Services.)
Vet Centers, which are located in most large cities, help veterans by providing counseling, employment help, and social services. Often they have family groups. They serve veterans who served during the Vietnam era or in Grenada, Lebanon, Panama, the Persian Gulf, or other areas of conflict.

Violent Crime Victims

National Organization for Victims' Assistance
307 West Seventh Street, Suite 1001
Fort Worth, TX 76102
(800) TRY-NOVA

This organization promotes public awareness of the problems of violent-crime victims, including rape victims. It also fights for victims' rights. They will provide referrals for help in the areas where individual callers live.

National Victim Center
2111 Wilson Boulevard, Suite 300
Arlington, VA 22201
(800) FYI-CALL

The National Victim Center was established in 1985 to advocate for victims' rights and for services, programs, and policy development. They have a legislative database, a resource library, and put out a list of their publications.

Rape Crisis Hotline
(800) 656-HOPE
Funded by the Rape, Abuse, and Incest Network (RAIN), this hotline operates 24 hours a day and can make referrals to local rape crisis centers.

Victims of Violence
151 Slater Street
Ottawa, Ontario
Canada K1P 5H3
(800) 267-5183
This international nonprofit group advocates for crime victims and provides referrals to sources of local help.

For Further Reading

The following books will provide further information on post-traumatic stress disorder.

Flannery, Raymond B. *Post Traumatic Stress Disorder: The Victim's Guide to Healing and Recovery.* New York: Crossroad, 1992.
Hybels-Steer, Mariann. *Aftermath: Survive and Overcome Trauma.* New York: Simon & Schuster, 1995.
Matsakis, Aphrodite. *I Can't Get Over It: A Handbook for Trauma Survivors.* Oakland, California: New Harbinger, 1992.
Terr, Lenore. *Too Scared to Cry: How Trauma Affects Children . . . and Ultimately Us All.* New York: Basic Books, 1990.

INDEX

Italic numbers indicate illustrations.